The Practicing Congregation

The Practicing Congregation

Imagining a New Old Church

Diana Butler Bass

THE
ALBAN
INSTITUTE

Herndon, Virginia

www.alban.org

Cover design: Adele Robey, Phoenix Graphics
Cover art: Leonard Freeman, "Lord Build This House"; used by permission of the artist. For more information, see p. 127.

Library of Congress Cataloging-in-Publication Data

Bass, Diana Butler, 1959–
  The practicing congregation : imagining a new old church / Diana Butler Bass.
    p. cm.
  Includes bibliographical references.
  ISBN 1-56699-305-9
  1. Church renewal. I. Title.

  BV600.3.B38 2004
  250'.973—dc22

                              2004016415

08   07   VG   5   6   7   8   9   10

For Dorothy Bass and Julie Ingersoll

Contents

Foreword

With each of her books, Diana Butler Bass is probing more deeply into what is going on in the world of religion and its institutional structures as the twenty-first century begins.

Her gift is to be able to look at the phenomena, the "things" of religion—numbers of people, finances, programs, creeds—and point to their deeper meanings. In doing so, she is unwilling to let us settle for the quick answers of the church-craft entrepreneurs, the ones with a point of view that fits into a neat package of conferences or the other snake-oil salespersons who have the newest gadget that will fix arteriosclerosis of the stewardship program or the vacuum of the evangelism effort. She sees those needs, but she sees beyond them.

Partly, I think it is that she is trying to see the story behind it all, the way improbable elements that rationally cannot coexist actually *do* exist very gracefully in plain congregations all across the land. She is interested in what congregations *do*, what they talk about and celebrate, not the things the pundits consider to be the Big Issues.

In looking for story and narrative, Diana Bass has discovered an unexplored territory overlooked by those looking for the dramatic or the "newsworthy." She finds an increasing instance of plain congregations focusing on their life and worship, learning to pray together and care for one another. She discovers new dimensions of

hospitality and Sabbath-celebration. She finds congregations using their imaginations to leap beyond what one might expect—
indeed, to do the impossible.

Her most prophetic efforts point beyond the polarizations
beloved of wise commentators, posing some new categories by
which to identify what is happening. In the push-and-pull of the
power of tradition and the impulse for change, she suggests that
perhaps there are congregations attempting to move beyond "establishment" to "intentionality."

The Practicing Congregation explodes the simplicity of the liberal–conservative polarization we have lived with for decades, and
proposes new ways of configuring the dynamics that drive religious life among us today and that are shaping our institutional
frameworks—deregulated and detraditionalized as they are. Diana
Butler Bass gives us new categories not only for thinking about
our institutional quandaries, but also for reconfiguring our language about life's spiritual and religious dimensions.

Speed Leas, my wise colleague who became the guru *par excellence* of church conflict, always told me that the most important
thing in working in a hot fight is to recognize that everybody
wants to simplify the issues so you have clear reasons for killing
each other (spiritually, of course, in *most* church conflicts). He said
that the most important thing one can do is to "complexify things."

What he meant, I think, is that only when you begin to see new
dimensions of what is going on are you able to get beyond dead
ends. When you see all ten sides of the issue you'd mistakenly
thought had only two, only then can you begin working out of the
polarization.

This book will help you broaden your ideas beyond the ones you
bring to it. It will help you complexify what you know and it will enrich your understanding. It will challenge your imagination.

I can't wait to see what she takes on next.

Loren B. Mead

Preface

Although interested Jews, Roman Catholics, and evangelical Protestants will find much here that resonates with their own experiences in faith communities, this book is directed to mainline Protestants because it is part of a larger study exploring mainline Protestant congregational vitality. The Project on Congregations of Intentional Practice, which I direct, is a three-year study of the role of Christian practices in fostering congregational vitality as experienced in churches of the historic mainline. The project is located at the Virginia Theological Seminary in Alexandria, Virginia, the largest seminary in the Episcopal Church, and is funded by Lilly Endowment Inc.

The project has identified fifty congregations that have experienced renewed senses of identity, vocation, and mission through intentionally embracing particular Christian practices that, in special ways, embodied a way of life that made sense of the Gospel in their unique cultural contexts. The congregations come from the major mainline denominations: the Evangelical Lutheran Church in America, the Presbyterian Church (USA), the United Methodist Church, the Episcopal Church, the United Church of Christ, the Disciples of Christ, and the Reformed Church in America. The churches are large, medium, and small, geographically spread, have male and female pastors, and are diverse in terms of class, race, and ethnicity. Theologically, they represent the "center" to the "left" of their traditions (on the assumption that vital conservative churches have been well studied). From these fifty participating churches, the project chose ten as ethnographic research sites in which research team members spent time worshiping, playing, praying, and listening.

This book, developed at an early stage of the project, drew data and insights from the congregations (and from some of my previous work in congregational studies) and used a variety of theoretical approaches to analyze what the research team heard and observed in the first phase. By appropriating theory from a number of disciplines and sources, it lays out a suggestive interpretation of contemporary mainline Protestantism that differs from the interpretations currently employed in most scholarly, journalistic, and religious circles. We hope that the project and this book will open some new and lively conversations around these issues. By laying out these theories at this stage of the project, we envision conversation as part of the research itself—as the ensuing discussion develops, deepens, and sharpens the ideas presented herein and as more field data enriches and clarifies the patterns suggested in these pages. Thus, this book should not be regarded as a closed case. Rather, it is an invitation into a conversation circle of experience, reflection, and imagination. More specifics about the project can be found at the Web site, http://www.practicingcongregations.org.

My warmest thanks go to the pastors and congregants of the participating congregations—without them and their vision, creativity, and imagination, there would be no story to tell. I am deeply grateful to Craig Dykstra, Christopher Coble, and John Wimmer at Lilly Endowment Inc. for financial, intellectual, and personal support of this project.

Also, I thank the project advisory board—Stephanie Paulsell, Anthony Robinson, Patrick Henry, Lee Ramsey, Eugene Sutton, Tim Shapiro, Robert Tate, Lisa Hess, Gary Erdos, and John Janka—for their incredible wisdom, able leadership, and thoughtful engagement with the ideas presented herein. And, most especially, I am grateful for their taking time out from their busy schedules to assist me on this project. Several friends, not formally associated with this project, have been conversation partners over the years and enlarged my own field of vision. These include Julie Ingersoll, Jonathan Wilson, Phyllis Tickle, Nancy Ammerman, Bill Sachs, Wade Clark Roof, Dorothy Bass, and Nora Gallagher. Many in this long list read chapters—making helpful and insightful comments along the way. Thanks to Loren Mead and Brian McLaren for writing the foreword and afterword that frame this book.

The project experiences daily community of scholarship and spirituality at the gentle precincts of Virginia Theological Seminary, whose administration, staff, faculty, and students are deeply committed to faith as a way of life. This project is richer because of campus-wide friendships that have formed around its vision, ideas, and passions. My gratitude goes out to all of you. Special thanks to my Christian Practices and Congregational Vitality class, and to seminary colleagues, coworkers, and students, especially Martha Horne, Mary Hix, Olivine Pilling, Bridget Smiley, Barney Hawkins, Jeff Hensley, Tim Sedgwick, Kathy Staudt, Judy Fentress-Williams, Roger Ferlo, Scott and Ardele Walters, Megan Stewart-Sicking, and Jennifer McKenzie.

I thank the publishing division of the Alban Institute, especially Richard Bass, David Lott, and Lisa Kinney Colburn, for all their support of my work on Christian practices and congregational vitality—and for their own work on the subject as well. It is a gift to write in community with people who share my hopes. And thanks to other friends at Alban, including Jim Wind, Ian Evison, John Janka, Kathryn Palen, Claudia Greer, Jacqui Lewis, and board president Pierce Klemmt, who more than put up with their colleague's wife!

Without the help of two men, this book would not exist. Joseph Stewart-Sicking serves as the project's research associate, primary interlocutor, intellectual colleague, lunch buddy, spiritual friend, and technology guru. When he eventually moves on to his own teaching and research career, I will feel like I have lost a limb. He deserves credit as the co-author of chapter 4, "Practice

Makes Pilgrims," and the sole author of the chart found in that chapter. He also prepared the Questions for Reflection and Study at the end of the book. Richard Bass, the director of publishing at the Alban Institute and my husband, is my constant companion in shaping my ideas, sharpening my insights, and sharing my experiences. In a very real way, he *made* this book happen—particularly when I was tempted to abandon it. I hope it honors his deep commitment to both me and the project.

In addition to Richard, I thank my daughter, Emma ("Mommy, are you writing *another* book?"), and my stepson, Jonah. Although I hope you will embrace your parents' faith as your own, I also pray that you will also feel free to reform your parents' church and never settle for the spiritual vision of the generation that went before.

Finally, this book is dedicated to two women who study, teach, and write about American religion—my sister-in-law, Dorothy Bass, and my best friend, Julie Ingersoll, both of whom have opened the door of life, faith, vocation, and vision for me many times. You are amazing teachers, and I have learned from both of you. Thank you.

The Practicing Congregation

Introduction

Straining after Images

Many books about mainline Protestantism argue for change—how mainline congregations must change, how to facilitate change, or how to manage change. As such, they offer programs and processes to move congregations ahead and help pastoral leaders change the communities they serve.

This book does not argue that mainline churches should change. Rather, it argues that mainline churches *are* changing and have *already* changed. It offers no program to make change happen in congregations. Instead, it attempts to track the changes—*where* the changes fit in the overall history of American religion, *what* cultural trends sparked the changes, *why* these things are happening now, and *how* mainline churches are experiencing new vitality through innovative engagement with traditional Christian practices. It also argues that a new kind of mainline congregation—*the practicing congregation*—has been born because of these changes. Practicing congregations weave together Christian practices—activities drawn from the long Christian tradition—into a pattern of being church that forms an intentional way of life in community.

As part of a pattern, these Protestant communities' micro-stories point toward an emerging congregational pattern in American religion and reflect larger spiritual, religious, and cultural concerns at the beginning of the twenty-first century: The edge of a trend whereby religious communities focus on meaning-making by gathering up the past and re-presenting it through both story and action in ways that help people connect with God, one another, and the world outside the doors of church buildings. Because it attempts to describe both the pattern of practicing congregations and the trend this congregational form represents, this book is an exercise in Christian cultural criticism—an attempt to read and narrate an aspect of American society through the informed lenses of religious studies, history of Christianity in America, and theological imagination.

In the *Republic,* Plato wrote, "I strain after images." According to theologian Margaret Miles, Plato "defined philosophy as the search for images that give a more or less adequate picture of the world in which human beings live [and] relate to one another" that draws both the "big picture" and "the delicate shade of nuance."[1] In the pages that follow, readers will not find a how-to program to create vital congregations. What unfolds here is a set of images that provides vision—a way of seeing something that is already happening in congregations across the country. Therefore, this book is an invitation into a different way of envisioning American Protestantism, its responses to larger cultural issues, its recent past, and its potential futures.

These chapters also reflect my own straining after images. As a churchgoer and a scholar, I find almost all the images of contemporary American Protestantism inadequate. Too often, what Protestants read about their tradition is ultimately unimaginative—the same tired story lines about conflict, about liberal and conservative divides, and about mainline decline. Contemporary mainline Protestants have believed these stories, allowing their self-understanding to be colonized by storytellers outside their tradition whose work is sometimes driven by agendas that benefit from stories of conflict and decline. By believing others' stories and not having the confidence to imagine their own narratives, mainline Protestants have often fuelled the cycle of conflict and given into the temptation of spiritual despair.

In these pages, I attempt to tell a story from *within* mainline tradition—one that examines recent evidence, employs more nuanced intellectual categories, and presents a more textured analysis than much of what I read and hear from other sources. The narratives and theories knit together here have convinced me that mainline churches can be envisioned more imaginatively by providing a different set of categories through which church leaders and congregants can see their experiences, hopes, and dreams reflected. And, I hope, that my own straining after images will open the way to others to use their imagination to understand their congregations—to see anew their challenges and surprising creativity.

In his article, "The Pastoral Imagination," Craig Dykstra argues that "pastoral ministry may require a complexity and integrity of intelligence that is as sophisticated as that needed for any kind of work we could think of."[2] The capacities called for in ministry include a variety of leadership, interpersonal, and theological skills. But, as Dykstra insists, in addition to this more readily available training, "good pastors also must have clear awareness and analytical understanding of the world that the church exists to serve, both locally and in relationship to the larger environment in which it operates."[3] Thus, as he defines it, the "pastoral imagination, a way of seeing into and interpreting the world" reaches from the inner places of the human heart, through the congregation, out to the world, and back again. The pastoral imagination allows us to envision God's presence in the world, to see the Spirit at work, to embody beauty, peace, hope, and faith in the midst of chaos, contingency, questioning, and despair.

I think Dykstra is quite correct about the pastoral imagination. However, the pastoral imagination is but one aspect of a larger calling of theological imagination, a spiritual gift imparted to the whole of God's people through baptism and the work of the Holy Spirit as part of the church's shared priesthood. Thus, the pastoral imagination works in tandem with something else— the congregational imagination, the imagination of God's people in community. The pastoral imagination and the congregational imagination are two different angles of vocational calling and

vision, one from the pulpit and the other from the pew, of a common spiritual gift of seeing God at work and embodying faith,
hope, and love in the world. In this book, I encourage mainline
Protestants to embrace the Spirit's gift of imagination by enlarg-
ing their field of vision. I urge readers to see beyond the walls of
their own church buildings in order to understand their sacred
location in both the longer story of American religious history
and the contemporary quest for spiritual meaning.

Without this enlarged field of vision, technical training in
theology and leadership amounts to little more than professional
expertise that may ensure excellent preaching, successful stewardship campaigns, and friendly newcomer programs. But such
expertise, while beneficial, does not spark the theological imagination to the deeper levels of meaning that come through knowing one's place in history and having a powerful sense of vocation
in a world that needs grace and mercy. Sometimes the technical
tools of leadership have, ironically, secularized the understanding of the ministry—both the ordained ministry and the one shared
by all the baptized. By seeing church as a business to be managed
or a patient to be healed, pastors and congregations allow themselves to be defined by worldviews, programs, and systems not
conversant with their own stories. James Hopewell, in his seminal
book *Congregation,* identified this as a shortfall in the life of faith
communities: "Rather than reduce its self-image to that of a machine
or an organism, the congregation might begin to give account of
itself as the full, storied household the Bible promises it can be."[4]

This book does not eschew the value of secular and
nontheological disciplines. But it seeks to interweave academic
and technical insights in the service of the theological imagination in its layered practices of pastoral *and* congregational imagination—and, in the process, add to an ongoing conversation
about the nature of religious leadership. My approach to this is
both rigorously learned and unabashedly confessional. Through
it all, I aspire to imaging American Protestantism truthfully
and with great hope—both its big picture and its delicate shades
of nuance.

Chapter One

A New Old Church

C hurch of the Epiphany, an Episcopal congregation three blocks from the White House in downtown Washington, D.C., was founded as a "city mission" in 1842. Throughout its long history, Epiphany has embodied the flow of American mainline history—antebellum volunteerism and reformism, tensions and divisions around the Civil War, the Social Gospel, establishment triumphalism, God-and-country fervor, missionary ecumenism, travail around civil rights and Vietnam, the impact of feminist and gay rights movements, and, eventually, decline. By 1992, 150 years after its founding, not many people remained in the decaying old urban building and a dwindling endowment paid the bills. There was talk around the diocese of closing it or combining it with another parish.

Ten years later, at the church's 160th anniversary, no one even whispered of closing Epiphany. Although not a big church—and certainly not a prestigious one—Epiphany bustles with new vitality. During the week, the church offers concerts, daily Eucharist, labyrinth walks, and adult spirituality courses for downtown workers. On Sundays, the 8:00 AM service welcomes two hundred homeless guests to both Eucharist and breakfast. The more traditional 11:00 AM service no longer comprises Washington's political elite and genteel aristocrats. Gone are the white-gloved acolytes and massive paid choir. Rather, a congregation of incredible diversity with multiple races, ethnicities, classes, generations, and sexual orientations now inhabits its pews. Their bills are paid through surprisingly generous congregational stewardship (the typical pledge at Epiphany is nearly twice the national average). They sing their songs to God guided by Taizé music, gospel songs and spirituals, Bach cantatas, Native American and African chants, and Anglican hymns.

Despite all the changes, Epiphany remains faithful to its mainline heritage. Its people speak the languages of social justice, inclusion, women's rights, ecumenism, and interreligious dialogue. They cherish their past commitment to the civil rights and peace movements of the 1960s; they proudly claim the first woman president of the House of Deputies (one of two national legislative bodies for the Episcopal Church) as one of their own. However, the old language has a new accent. The privatized piety of old-style Protestant liberalism has been supplanted by a new sense of spiritual vitality and expressive faith. People these days practice healing prayer, hospitality, silence, discernment, stewardship, and peacemaking; they attend retreats, quiet days, spirituality workshops, and Bible studies. These practices happen purposefully, intentionally chosen by a new generation of churchgoers who share and teach them in community. Although Epiphany's changes occurred in fits and starts, alternating between conflict and graceful acceptance, people have been learning a new way of life together. No longer does the congregation depend on a liberal "prince of the pulpit" to direct its common life. No more do they depend upon the nursery for future members. They are learning to open doors, reach out, and bring people in.

In the last decade, Epiphany did not reject its mainline Protestant past. A palpable sense of justice activism and civic responsibility is still prominent, but a new sense of worship, spiritual depth, and seriousness regarding liturgy and the Christian scriptures now exists here—a growing, emotive, transcendent, and communal religiosity. It is as if the congregation took the bags of its ancestors, journeyed out of their parents' (and grandparents') house of mid-twentieth-century mainline Protestantism, and entered a new theological world—a world shaped by a renewed interest in scripture and Christian practices. In that place, Epiphany is finding new life.

Through its 160 years of existence, Church of the Epiphany has typified American mainline religion. Once Episcopalians were so dominant in Washington that an entire book—*The Power of Their Glory*—was written, extolling the ways in which the denomination informally controlled the city's social and political life.[1] Although it sits so close to the White House, Epiphany no longer serves as establishment religion. Long gone are the days of Episcopal glory. Like much of the old mainline, Church of the Epiphany has been relegated to the margins of Washington's power.

Instead of simply grieving over the loss, however, Epiphany is finding new power—the power that can only be found when, as Jesus promised, "one loses his life for my sake." Down the long, hard slide from the pinnacle of establishment prominence, Epiphany has discovered that cultural marginalization, peeling paint, urban funkiness, global diversity, homeless congregants, and healing prayer are gifts from a generous God. Epiphany's pilgrimage, however, raises a question: Might this congregation be but one example of something that is beginning to happen across American mainline Protestantism?

Yesterday's News

In the last three decades, the story of American mainline Protestantism was rewritten. Once considered the very definition of American religion, a host of late twentieth-century social trends and historical movements assailed venerable traditions of Protestant churchgoing, making mainline religion increasingly outmoded in a pluralistic and post-Christian society.[2] These old-line churches lost the cultural power, prestige, and influence they previously wielded. Scholars identified, studied, analyzed, and debated the patterns of and reasons for the changes and the increasing irrelevance of America's historic mainline denominations.[3] Mainline Protestantism—including the story of its decline—became a sidebar in the epic of American religious pluralism, the growth of fundamentalism and evangelicalism, and the emergence of secular postmodernism.[4]

Mainline Protestants neither expected nor welcomed these changes. This cultural displacement forced them to focus inward and deal with issues of identity, vision, resources, and organization—often with great conflict and smothering self-doubt. But conflict and internal questioning signaled something more than just anger or confusion; they indicated that unnoticed creativity and innovation were at work in unexpected places in the old mainline. "Chaos often breeds life," wrote Henry Adams in 1906, "when order breeds habit." In the last decades of the twentieth century, mainline churches were being forced to break old habits.

Thirty years removed from the initial studies of mainline ennui, the most precipitous drops seem now to be ending and these denominations may be entering, however tentatively, into a new period of their history.[5] In some cases, numerical decreases have slowed or stopped, mainline church attendance appears to be rising, mainline theology is demonstrating new sophistication, and higher levels of commitment and giving are beginning to register among the laity. Quietly, without much attention from either an uninterested public or skeptical scholars, reports of emerging vitality are being heard across the old mainline.[6]

While academics and pundits have made much of the decline, far fewer studies have appeared accounting for the reorganization and revitalization of old mainline churches such as Washington's Church of the Epiphany. Sociologists Nancy Ammerman, Jackson Carroll, C. Kirk Hadaway, Donald Miller, Wade Clark Roof, David Roozen, and Robert Wuthnow have offered studies suggesting the development of new styles of congregational life in American mainline religion.[7] Yet, despite their work identifying nascent patterns of vitality, other scholars, the media, and critics have not paid attention to the emerging creativity and new congregational experiments in mainline Protestantism. Stories about American religion tend toward the exotic (typically about the growth of Eastern religion), conflict (usually about women's issues or homosexuality), or the fanatical (fundamentalism of all sorts). Mainline churches rarely make news unless the story involves sex, scandal, or corruption.

The problem is not the lack of ability or even interest on the part of many writers to tell new stories about American Protestantism. The problem is that many observers have neither closely examined the decline theories (largely accepting them as fact) nor paid serious attention to the styles and patterns of religious life and spirituality in mainline churches that are now emerging in what appears to be a *post*-decline period. That is the *new* news: American mainline Protestantism is changing—maybe more than it has in a century. And those changes are part of a much larger story about religious life and spirituality in contemporary America—the patterns and trends that are shaping the way in which future generations will experience the Protestant faith, one of the most venerable forms of American religion.

New Wineskins: Practicing Congregations

When I was a student at a Christian college in the 1970s, I took a class on "contemporary ministry" in which we read a then-recently published book, *The Problem of Wineskins*. The author, Howard Snyder, claimed, "In our fast-changing world fewer and fewer people are interested in a pile of old wineskins, no matter how well-preserved they may be."[8] He further argued that American Protestant churches—evangelical and liberal ones—needed both the "new wine" of Jesus *and* "new wineskins" of congregational change in order to meet the challenges of a post-Christian culture.

In the 1970s, the impulse for change prompted a host of innovative congregational experiments. Mainline Protestants might title the twenty-five years following the appearance of Snyder's book as *The Experiment with Wineskins*. During the last decades of the twentieth century, theologians, sociologists, and church-growth theorists suggested, promoted, and implemented a variety of ways to become new wineskins—suggesting a variety of strategies for mainline renewal and hoping each new program would solve problems associated with the decline. An almost-dizzying array of styles and approaches has developed—from house churches and seeker services and megachurches to café churches and online communities—as potential new forms and patterns that foster congregational vitality.[9]

Although they take numerous specific forms, these patterns could be grouped according to three different revitalization types: the conservative-evangelical type, the new-paradigm type, and the diagnostic type. And the contours of each of these types emerged about the same time Snyder's book was written—in the 1970s. Clearly, this concurrent longing for vital and authentic Christian community signaled the start of a creative new period in Protestant congregational experimentation.

Beginning with researcher Dean Kelley's work in 1972, some people suggested that only theologically conservative churches—those that offered "high demand" religion—would grow and initiated a host of evangelical and charismatic renewal movements across mainline denominations.[10] Others, inspired by the marketing success of Willow Creek Community Church in South Barrington, Illinois, imitated that congregation's "seeker strategy" to woo religiously disenfranchised baby boomers into symbolically and denominationally neutral megachurches that constituted a "new paradigm" of church life.[11] And some leaders, notably Loren Mead of the Alban Institute, sensed that the only hope for the mainline could be found in vital congregations, and suggested that traditional churches needed a kind of diagnostic fix, skills borrowed from the social and therapeutic sciences—in systems and structures, conflict management, and leadership theory—to develop a healthy corporate identity and clearer vision for vocation. Healthy congregations, like healthy individuals, would grow and live into God's fullest potential for them.[12]

Each of the above types of renewal (sometimes singly and sometimes in combination) has been successful in some mainline congregations. However, not one of them explains the transformation at Church of the Epiphany in Washington, D.C. Epiphany is not theologically conservative; it does not minimize its theological distinctiveness in architecture, liturgy, or denominational identity. Although it has used diagnostic strategies to aid with particular problems, the fundamental changes at Epiphany were not primarily systemic or managerial. Epiphany has been changing *theologically and spiritually*—undergoing a transformation in content, practice, and worldview. Those changes are continuous with its past, but they also represent a new way of being mainline church. Indeed, the experience of Epiphany—as well as of other congregations—seems to suggest that an additional pattern appears to have quietly emerged, and has been largely unnoticed as a locus of Protestant vitality: *an intentional and practicing congregation*.[13] Among the numerous possibilities of congregational reorganization, this pattern may well be what one of my friends refers to as the "most faithful and most hopeful" for renewed mainline vitality.

Many congregations could rightly be considered intentional in some manner and engage in practices conducive to their mission. For example, many new-paradigm churches are quite intentional—and even use the language of "intention," "purpose," or "practice" to describe their vocation and mission. However, most of the practices engaged by new-paradigm churches tend to be contemporary in nature, and are typically entrepreneurial, market based—defining faith as a consumer product—and technique oriented. At the same time, the message of new-paradigm churches remains theologically evangelical or conservative.[14] Some scholars have suggested that new-paradigm churches actually represent a new phase in the history of American congregations. However, with their distinctive appeal to early baby boomers and their overall comfort with consumerist culture, it seems more appropriate to classify them as the final development of congregational styles that emerged in the late 1970s and early 1980s. Indeed, the May 2004 newsletter *Religion Watch* noted the decline of interest among younger Americans for "baby boomer-led megachurches and their programmed, entertainment-based approach" in favor of small to medium-sized congregations with more liturgical forms of worship.[15]

Whatever their seeming similarities, however, mainline practicing congregations like Church of the Epiphany reflect elements

of new-paradigm congregations but typically *invert* their characteristics. The emerging mainline congregations have theologically
moderate-to-liberal messages (for example, they typically believe
that the Bible is primarily story, myth, or allegory; they accept the
consequences of religious and racial pluralism and multiculturalism, believing in an explicit or implicit universalism; they
support expanded leadership roles for women and demonstrate
higher tolerance toward gay and lesbian members) *but* they have
embraced traditional Christian practices in worship, prayer, moral
formation, and life together.

Practicing congregations experience new vibrancy through a
reappropriation of historic Christian practices and a sustained communal engagement with Christian narrative. These congregations
may be described as

> Communities that choose to rework denominational tradition in
> light of local experience to create a web of practices that transmit
> identity, nurture community, cultivate mature spirituality, and
> advance mission. These practices—as varied as classical spiritual
> disciplines such as *lectio divina* and centering prayer, or moral
> and theological practices like householding, Sabbath keeping, for-
> giveness, doing justice, and hospitality—are drawn from, recover,
> or reclaim individual and corporate patterns of historic Christian
> living that provide meaning and enliven a sense of spiritual con-
> nection to God and others. In these congregations, transmission
> of identity and vocation does not occur primarily through famil-
> ial religious tradition, civic structures, or the larger culture. Chris-
> tian identity is neither assumed nor received. Rather, transmission
> occurs through choice, negotiation, and reflexive theological en-
> gagement, in community, by adopting a particular way of life as
> expressed by and sustained through historically grounded Chris-
> tian practices.[16]

While other types of congregations were birthed in the 1970s,
practicing congregations seem to have emerged around 1990. Earlier congregational experiments mirror the cultural anxiety and issues of the 1960s and 1970s. Practicing congregations also reflect

those mid-century concerns (many of which are still having a profound impact on American life) and build on the fruitful congregational experimentation of earlier forms. In addition, however, they appear to be responding to more recent changes in American religion, specifically new impulses in Protestant theology and new longings for faith-filled meaning-making in post-Christian culture.

A New Kind of Congregation

So, what is happening at Church of the Epiphany? What does its new place in Washington's religious economy say about larger possibilities for understanding the story of American mainline Protestantism? How does the development of this congregational type enrich or enlarge our understanding of American religion?

In his essay "Toward a History of American Congregations," historian E. Brooks Holifield proffers a periodization scheme of congregational history.[17] Typically, clergy and scholars think of history in terms of a *single* congregation. They know that a church's history is important for understanding its current needs and vision, its conflicts and challenges. However, few people consider that congregational history is not simply the local and particular. Single congregations, at various moments in their corporate life, respond to larger social and cultural trends.

In his chronology of congregational history, Holifield describes the characteristics of successive generations of American congregations—characteristics that reflect the social and cultural ethos in which *all* American congregations exist—and argues that all congregations are microcosms in which the larger social trends unfold. He identifies four distinctive patterns of congregational organization through American history: *comprehensive congregations*, 1607–1789; *devotional congregations*, 1789–1870; *social congregations*, 1870–1950; and *participatory congregations*, 1950–present (see chart, p. 17).

According to Holifield, *comprehensive congregations* understood their mission as a call to serve all the people in a particular geographical community, and they were supported by the state for that very purpose. These were "town-square churches" in which membership and colonial citizenship were equated.

Devotional congregations, born in the fierce religious competitiveness of the young nation, had to attract members to a denomination by providing innovative and distinctive worship practices. These churches emphasized personal and social salvation in the form of voluntary associations that they believed would bring forth God's kingdom in America.

Social congregations of the late nineteenth century returned to the ideal of comprehensiveness, but these churches could no longer embrace an entire town or city. Instead, they became denominational "homes" for members in a particular area and initiated an array of programs to meet the religious and social needs of a changing society. In these churches, the parish hall became the most important sacred space on their property (churches did not have parish halls before this time; they only had sanctuaries). Such all-purpose rooms, typically with fireplaces, kitchens, and homey furnishings, served as the congregation's parlor for family events.

Participatory congregations of the post–World War II period retained the "full-service" ideal of social congregations but, instead of depending on denomination or geography to provide members, these churches developed innovative worship and new programs as evangelism tools for recruiting new members. No longer did they simply seek to serve the local community; rather, they created targeted programs to attract people or address particular problems. The programmatic strategies employed by these congregations tended to be market oriented—defining faith as a product and congregants as religious consumers. By responding to the religious "market," they created what Holifield calls "cultural comprehensiveness," deeply complex congregations that are, essentially, "a group of groups."[19] In essence, these decentralized churches functioned as a kind of religious shopping mall to meet the faith needs of certainty, health, prosperity, or security of religious consumers. In style (but not necessarily in their theological content), participatory congregations comfortably reflected the surrounding culture.

A History of American Congregations, 1607–Present[18]

Years/Type	Setting	Reach/Audience	Entrance	Primary Orientations	Church & Society
1607–1789 Comprehensive Congregations	*Colonial* Established Church	Geographical Churched	Birthright	· Education · Information · Public Square	Membership=Citizenship Tension: None (except dissenting groups: high)
1789–1870 Devotional Congregations	*New Republic* Democratic Protestant Diversity	Denominational Small Town, Rural Churched, Unchurched	Recruitment Evangelism	· Worship · Salvation · Personal Piety	Voluntary Associations Christian America Tension: Medium
1870–1950 Social Congregations	*Industrial America* Democratic Protestant Empire	Denominational Urban Churched	Birthright Denominationalism	· Home · Family · Parish Hall	Church *is* a civic organization Tension: None/low (except immigrant groups: high)

1950–current
Participatory Congregations
Variants
· Seeker Churches
· Program/Corporate
· [New Paradigm: hinge form]
	Post-WWII
	Democratic
	Religious Pluralism
	Consumerist
		Muted Denominationalism;
		Nondenominational
		Suburban
		Churched, Unchurched,
		Returnees, Switchers
			Niche Marketing
			"Full Service" Attraction
			Evangelism
			Personal Conversion
				· Experiential
				· Programs
				· Group of Groups
				· Decentralized &
				  Democratized
				· Shopping Mall or
				  "Box Store"
					Individuals or interest groups engage civic arena through policy, politics, or system change
					Tension: Medium–low to medium

1990–current Intentional Congregations Variants (major) · [New Paradigm: hinge form] · Practicing Congregations · Emergent Church	*Postmodern* Democratic Fragmentation "Multivocal" Creative	Post-traditional;Retraditioned Denominationalism;Traditioned Nondenominationalism Churched, Switchers, Unchurched, Post-churched, "Tourists"	Hospitality Open Sacraments Multiportal	· Worship · Way of Life · Practices · Spirituality · Formation	Theological critique of culture Hands-on service; social action; justice Tension: Medium-high to high

Of the types of congregational vitality discussed above, the conservative-evangelical type, the new-paradigm type, and the diagnostic type generally fit Holifield's periodization under the rubric of participatory congregations, the organizational paradigm that dominated American religious life from 1950 to 1990.[20] *Practicing congregations,* however, do not fit the description of participatory congregations. As a type, it pushes beyond Holifield's chronology and suggests that something new may be happening in American Protestantism.

Placed historically, it seems that a new phase of Protestant congregational history may have opened around 1990 and is now in its earliest expression. I would like to suggest that practicing congregations are one distinct style of vitality under a larger rubric of congregational change—that of the *intentional congregation.* Intentional congregations (including the practicing congregation form) share some of the characteristics of participatory congregations, in that they possess a sense of dynamism, movement, fluidity, and flexibility in structure, leadership, shared ministry, and worship.

Yet intentional congregations resist the technique-oriented, program-driven, and therapeutic forms of participatory congregations as well as the marketing strategies employed by that model. Intentional congregations are highly tuned to spiritual authenticity and communal coherence; they construct faith primarily as a way of life in community.[21] Whereas participatory congregations generally reflect the larger culture in terms of style and language, intentional congregations distance themselves from surrounding values and self-describe in more theological, sacramental, mythical, and mystical terms. Intentional congregations tend toward a higher level of discomfort with their surroundings—particularly consumerist culture—and emphasize creativity and community more than organization and program.[22] And they are *not* primarily "posttraditional," as some observers argue. Rather, they might be best seen either as *retraditioned denominationalism* or as *traditioned nondenominationalism* as they seek to connect contemporary life to the longer practices and narratives of the Christian tradition in self-conscious and purposeful ways.

Practicing congregations are but one form—a distinctive mainline Protestant form—of congregational vitality under the larger historical rubric of the "intentional congregation." A recent study of the Church of England listed fifteen possible intentional forms of emerging congregational life.[23] And a survey of Catholic youth suggested that eight differing styles of communal gathering were developing among younger American Catholics.[24] Among American evangelicals, the intentional pattern comprises a complex set of forms roughly grouped as "emergent church" or "the younger evangelicals."[25]

Thus, two things are occurring simultaneously in American religion: First, a larger rubric of congregational organization is emerging—that of the intentional congregation; and second, the impulse toward intentionality is taking a variety of tradition-specific forms—none of which can be considered to be *the* dominant or singular pattern. At this point, American congregational life is like a mosaic. The large picture of intentionality can be discerned by standing back; the multiplicity of forms of the individual pieces is both beautiful in creativity and confusing up close! This mosaic of change is becoming an increasingly obvious phenomenon; however, it is only just substantial enough to be discerned and to be given shape and definition through language and narrative.

In the overall mosaic, intentional mainline churches *tend* to take the form of practicing congregations as described in the pages that follow. And, as will become obvious, "practicing" itself is a form with clusters of activities and a multiplicity of possibilities that make the pattern itself fluid and dynamic—a kind of mini-mosaic within the larger one. It may well be that this form of congregational vitality is most native to mainline Protestants, the pattern that grows from the soil of their experience, history, and traditions—thus constituting the "most faithful and most hopeful" possibility for renewal, vitality, growth, and spiritual and theological deepening.

Sadly, many mainline congregations and their national denominational structures continue to be controlled by the worldviews of either social or participatory churchgoing. Since these worldviews are passing and becoming increasingly less culturally tenable, institutions that cling to them will experience conflict and decline. Hence, the old story: "mainline decline." But around the edges of the old mainline, in communities that are practicing faith as a way of life, a new kind of grassroots congregation has embarked on pilgrimage.

The Protestant mainline is, to quote plague victims being hauled away to the graveyard in an old Monty Python movie, "not dead yet." Some congregations are sensing the cultural sea change and finding new ways of navigating their life together. In the process, they are experiencing unexpected vitality, theological deepening, and spiritual growth. Church of the Epiphany is one of those places—an old, establishment church in an establishment city—creating new ways of being authentically Christian in a post-Protestant, post-traditional, post-everything age.

Chapter Two

Just the Way It Is

Occasionally, a congregation asks me to consult with them during a time of conflict. Whatever the situation, however different this church is from others, one thing almost always remains the same—people want someone to blame for their troubles. "It is his fault," congregants will say of the new minister. "Everything was fine before he arrived." Perhaps it is the fault of "all those newcomers" or "the choir director." Whoever—or whatever—churchgoers blame for congregational turmoil, typically the troublemaker can be found within the building.

The same goes for denominational conflict—people blame internal factors for their struggles with change. Fault for denominational stress is placed on women's ordination, liberals or conservatives (depending upon the church) "taking over the seminaries," the new hymnal or liturgies, the rise of contemporary worship, or the election of a controversial leader. People tend to blame something *inside the denominational structures* for the tensions, pressures, and stresses associated with change in American churches.

In the midst of conflict, however, people often fail to recognize the obvious: What if no one can be blamed? What if no one is at fault? Many changes, conflicts, and tensions do not arise from factors within religious communities themselves. Rather, these things are the result of institutions reacting and responding to larger cultural changes—trends, ideas, and practices *outside the church building.* People bring their fears about large-scale social change with them to church. These cultural anxieties are often a hidden source of congregational conflict. Congregants overfocus on what is at hand and forget the stress and anxiety of global cultural changes that are affecting nearly every human being on the planet at this juncture of history.

The congregational experimentation in the 1970s and 1980s was the result of cultural shifts that occurred in the two decades immediately following World War II: the rise of the middle-class meritocracy, suburbanization, the birth of the baby boom genera-tion, expanded access to college and university education, the civil rights movement, feminism, Sunbelt immigration of whites and northern migration of blacks, and the turmoil over Vietnam. All these changes unhinged traditional American religious patterns and called for greater clarity about the Christian message and greater authenticity in Christian congregations. Some churches rose to the challenge, but many did not. In a wave of social change (and often unreflective resistance to it), many congregations lost their ability to retain younger members or attract new ones. Congrega-tions often suffered because of the gap that developed between their internal inherited practices and external cultural realities. And, more than occasionally, they suffered because their particular pat-tern of congregational life was considered coterminous with "Chris-tian tradition" or "orthodox faith," hence confusing a historical moment in American culture with theological vitality and scrip-tural truth. In short, many mid-twentieth-century churchgoers enshrined the pattern of social congregations as something akin to revealed truth!

In the 1980s, the gap between cultural change and congrega-tional life widened even further when the younger baby boomers and a new generation, GenX, entered adulthood. Their world was shaped by both the events of the 1960s *and* escalating cultural and technological change.[1] Many of these younger Americans grew up disengaged from any form of traditional faith community and their

worldviews differed sharply from those of their parents and grandparents regarding religious practice. While the previous generations' social churchgoing reigned as the dominant form of
establishment Protestantism, their children largely rejected that
style and its patterns of practice as irrelevant to their lives.[2] In the
last two decades of the twentieth century, as these people came of
age, two dramatic cultural impulses reshaped American religious
belief and spirituality: disestablishment and detraditionalization—
both of which had devastating effects on business-as-usual in mainline Protestantism.

Unlike the new minister, the newcomers, the choir director, or
the denominational bureaucrats, these cultural impulses are
nobody's fault. They are manifestations of global philosophies,
international capitalism, technological revolutions, and reorganized
political and social community. They are the most recent developments of centuries of Western history, political economy, and philosophy that now shape human culture on a massive international
scale. Who is to blame? Martin Luther? René Descartes? Adam
Smith? Thomas Jefferson? The Wright Brothers? Walt Disney? Standard Oil? Bill Gates? They are nobody's fault, and nobody is to
blame. They just are what they are. We cannot change them, we
cannot fix them, we cannot isolate ourselves from them, and we
cannot ignore them. They are the sea in which we all swim.

It is against this background, and in response to these changes,
that new expressions of congregational vitality, such as patterns of
intentional practice, are developing.

Disestablishment: Round Three

One of the most enduring and distinctive characteristics of American religion is that the federal government is constitutionally
forbidden to establish any form of national church. Radical at its
inception and a break from European tradition, the new United
States of America disestablished religion in 1789. Despite the historical act of disestablishment, scholars recognize that the separation of church and state did not occur in a single legal moment.

Rather, disestablishment is a process that occurred in three rough
stages whereby Americans continuously redefined "the relationship between religion and culture."[3]

In 1789, the *first disestablishment* formally and legally forbade
the federal government from creating or supporting a single national church. However, formal disestablishment initiated an *informal* religious establishment, a powerful cultural center of
interdenominational Protestantism that held sway intellectually and
socially for more than a century. As one historian wrote, "Protestants conceived of an American Christian democracy infused by
their church traditions . . . [Everything] was geared to protect white
Anglo-Saxon Protestant civilization. The arts, economics, politics,
even war, bore the Protestant imprint."[4]

In the early twentieth century, a *second disestablishment* challenged this informal Protestant establishment to include broader
freedoms and civic participation for Jews and Roman Catholics,
thus creating a kind of ethical establishment of "Judeo-Christian"
values in the "religious and cultural middle" of American public
life.[5] By the 1950s, sociologist Will Herberg identified a tripar-
tite religious ethos that comprised all in a single American faith:
"Protestant-Catholic-Jew."[6] Many churchgoers can still remem-
ber the second disestablishment and the shift away from a distinctly Protestant national identity to a Judeo-Christian one,
whereby a generalized sense of monotheistic faith replaced specific Protestant authority as the moral custodian of the nation. And
some Americans assume that this twentieth-century tradition still
oversees the nation's soul.

However, since the 1960s, a *third disestablishment* of religion
has been under way.[7] In this phase, all organized belief—especially
traditional Western religion—has been dislodged even as a custodian of national morality and ethics—replaced instead by the authority of the autonomous individual. The shift is easy to
understand. In the 1950s, one could appeal to "church" or "synagogue" and assume that ministers and rabbis held communal moral
authority. By the 1980s, however, that assumption had disappeared—one could no longer make moral claims on the basis of

"the Bible states," "the church teaches," or "rabbinic tradition says." Rather, individuals assumed that religious, moral, and ethical choices were internal and personal matters instead of external or institutional ones.

Today, when a person seeks answers for religious questions, he or she might turn to Oprah or Dr. Phil, browse the bookshelves at Barnes & Noble, consult a therapist, watch a television evangelist, engage a new spiritual practice (like yoga or meditation), ask a friend or neighbor, or cruise the Internet. He or she may read a Bible. Or maybe not. A seeker might ask a cleric—but of what religion?

Added to an increased sense of individual authority is a multiplicity of spiritual and religious choices not readily available to earlier generations of Americans. In one generation, what was once the white cultural mainstream has broadened to include numerous ethnic and racial minorities and the variety of faith traditions practiced in their communities. American culture has switched from a univocal culture (a relatively unified set of external authorities) to being a multivocal ("of many voices") religious society in which the individual is the final arbiter of truth. Thus, both personal autonomy and multiculturalism hastened the demise of the Caucasian Protestant-Catholic-Jew religious establishment.

American Protestants—and American congregations more generally—adjusted to each historical change of religious disestablishment. Around 1800, some Protestants feared that no state church would mean the death of Christian faith in the United States. However, they quickly shifted toward the voluntary principle in religion and reasserted cultural authority through informal channels. When that pattern no longer fit newer realities, American Protestants around 1900 again adapted—this time to include Jews and Catholics in a larger vision of moral practice and assumed that they could share civic space with biblically likeminded neighbors. Many twentieth-century Americans grew up with crosses, mangers, and menorahs in front of their town halls, with ministers, priests, and rabbis blessing public rituals.

In the last stage of disestablishment in the 1960s and 1970s, however, public religious expression shifted away from any form of state support for organized religion to the rights of free speech of individuals and protection of minority groups. While it is considered inappropriate (and unconstitutional) for a professional minister or a state-paid teacher to offer a prayer at school, an individual student may do so as an act of free speech. Thus, Americans still experience much public religion, but such speech and activity are no longer communally based, state supported, or denominational. Because it is individual, it is deeply pluralistic, preferring no faith, whether a majority or minority one, over another. Public religious acts are expressions of private opinions. And, because minority religions secured public space in this process, many alternative voices are now heard in the public square. America is now a multivocal religious culture.

This shift profoundly affects American congregations. For many Protestants, being exiled from civic space they once held in favor of personal freedom, individual autonomy, and religious multiculturalism has been a much more difficult adjustment task than some of the earlier phases of disestablishment.[8] Some, notably conservative evangelicals, have fought to "take back" America and reassert their authority in the public square. Mainline Protestants, on the other hand, sometimes ignore the changes and try to engage public life as their grandparents did. When old strategies fail, they most often bemoan the changes or retreat from civic engagement. Whether liberal or conservative, Protestant ministers sadly accept (and sometimes decry) the lack of their ministerial authority in this new culture. Thus, disestablishment affects the way churches practice public ministry—but more importantly, it affects the way that congregations see themselves and their larger mission to the world. For some, it has meant renewed zeal. For others, it underscores a painful sense of being lost in the universe.

The shift to individual autonomy, however, is not altogether a bad thing. It is, as stated above, just what it is. The shift is the most recent phase in a large historical process in which ideals originally proposed at the time of the Protestant Reformation are being worked out by successive generations. The upside of individual autonomy is that people must take spiritual, moral, and ethical responsibility for themselves, thus giving them a higher stake in their choices. When they join congregations or religious movements, they do so because they believe in them and find something congruent with their life experience in a particular gathering. In short, they are *potentially* more committed churchgoers when they walk in the door of a church than their parents, who (perhaps) remained faithful out of communal loyalty rather than personal choice.

It took awhile for local congregations to feel the reality of the third disestablishment. Until the 1980s or early 1990s, some mainline churches continued to imagine that they, regardless of what legal niceties or cultural trends dictated, were still in charge. These congregations felt entitled to cultural support for their message, for new members, and for money. This, of course, no longer held true in most regions of the country (the process of the "third disestablishment" has occurred at differing rates in the north and south and in urban and rural settings). Given a new set of historical circumstances, and a growing awareness of Protestant marginalization, a new kind of mainline congregation would have to develop that could function in relation to cultural repositioning.

Around 1990, two influential books appeared that pointed out the impact of the third disestablishment on Protestant congregations: *Resident Aliens* by Stanley Hauerwas and William Willimon and *The Once and Future Church* by Loren Mead.[9] These critics accused all types of participatory congregations of being inadequate in terms of depth—however "successful" they might be in terms of numbers or program—and believed their programmatic and organizational emphases to be a theological dead end, unable to provide authentically Christian ways of life in a post-Christian, postmodern society (the "third disestablishment" as described above). Each trumpeted the "end of Christendom" and mapped out possible futures for mainline Protestant congregations to *be* church and not the heirs of religious-cultural privilege. Mead, Hauerwas, Willimon, and others began to argue also that mainline churches would need to *work* to communicate

their message (and they might even have to figure it out first!)
and be clear about their identity and vocation in order to attract
and spiritually form new members from a variety of non-WASP con-
stituencies and from younger generations of Americans.

Detraditionalization: Is That a Real Word?

Not long ago, I wrote a book chapter in which I used the word
detraditionalization to describe issues related to church and state.
The book's editor called me on the telephone and asked, "Is that a
real word?"

"Yes," I laughed. "It's a sociological term for post-traditional
society and culture. Usually, I don't find such jargon-like terms
helpful. But this one explains a lot."

Detraditionalization is a set of processes, variously described
as "post-traditional" or "postmodern," whereby received traditions no longer provide meaning and authority in everyday life.
Paul Heelas, a British sociologist defines it as follows:

> Detraditionalization involves a shift of authority: from "without"
> to "within." It entails the decline of the belief in pre-given or natu-
> ral orders of things. Individual subjects are themselves called upon
> to exercise authority in the face of the disorder and contingency
> which is thereby generated. "Voice" is displaced from established
> sources, coming to rest in the self.[10]

Wade Clark Roof and Jackson Carroll argue that in contemporary society all forms of tradition—especially religious traditions—are "caught up in major upheaval and transformation" in
which society suffers from "loss of habit and memory," where the
"force of tradition" no longer offers spiritual or personal security.
Accordingly, detraditionalization is felt at deep levels of personal
identity "as even the simplest of things we take for granted in everyday life are affected."[11]

The current form of religious disestablishment in the United
States is a particular North American political expression of a larger
global phenomenon: the *detraditionalization* of contemporary

societies. The shift of authority necessary to the third disestablishment manifests itself in all forms of cultural authority—from politics to morality to family to the church. Multivocal authority is fundamental to detraditionalization.

In earlier American history, congregations were carriers of tradition-informed culture, assuming, as Heelas says, "our way is the right way," in a hierarchically ordered society where "taken-for-grantedness" is fundamental to personal and community identity.[12] Establishment Protestantism as enshrined in the congregations of the 1950s was, according to these definitions, an institutional embodiment of traditionally informed American culture. Mainline churches of the post-World War II era assumed a "right" Protestant "way of life" based on family ties and upheld by the cultural supports of the state, the media, and, most especially, the public schools.

I was born into such a congregation: St. John's United Methodist Church in Baltimore, Maryland. There, photographs of the men's Bible study, dating back to the turn of the twentieth century, hung in the church basement; names of my ancestors filled the baptismal record in the pastor's office. In their turn, my parents assumed congregational leadership roles that their parents had once held—teaching their children lessons from the Bible and how to make a big enough casserole for the parish supper. My Girl Scout troop met in the room that also served as my Sunday school classroom, where mementoes of God and country decorated the walls—and where stories of both Abraham and Abraham Lincoln shaped young congregants in an American Protestant way of life. My parents did not invent this way of life. Rather, they inhabited patterns that had been passed to them from their parents and their parents before them. They were simply passing those patterns on to their children.

Something, however, did not work. It did not "take." They did not realize that this way of life would lose its credibility when challenged by technological change, global communications, religious pluralism, expanded higher education, geographic mobility, and international capitalism. My parents' world was a *closed culture*, a world embraced by the manners, mores, and habits of working-class Baltimore. My world, however, was not a closed culture; it would be a *negotiated world* emerging from decisions and choices I would have to make. Because of larger cultural changes, I developed ways to critique the world of St. John's United Methodist Church. I would eventually have to decide what I believed true from that old universe and how it could be put into practice in a new one.

My experience testifies to the detraditionalization of our culture. "Detraditionalization entails," Heelas explains, "that people have acquired the opportunity to stand back from, critically reflect upon, and lose their faith in what the tradition has to offer. They have to arrive at a position where they can *have their own say.*"[13] Theorists of detradtionalization argue that "organized culture—sustained voices of moral and aesthetic authority serving to differentiate values, to distinguish between what is important and what is not, to facilitate coherent, purposeful, identities, life-plans or habits of the heart—has disintegrated."[14] Thus, detraditionalization is not only a real word; it is the lived reality of millions of people in today's world.[15]

Detraditionalization has taken particular forms in the United States, but it is not a nationally confined phenomenon. Indeed, it is a global one. And most international tensions, conflicts, and terrorist movements can be understood in relation to detraditionalization. In this process, a culture shifts from univocality to multivocality—from a single source of meaning and authority to competing ones whereby individuals must choose the beliefs and authorities that frame their lives. In a detraditioned society, no priest, minister, rabbi, or mullah can decide for you.

Thus, while American and European Christians are struggling with faith in a post-Protestant—or post-Christendom—cultural context, Muslims in the Middle East are struggling over whether to enforce the univocality of Islamic statehood or to embrace the plurality of religious freedom and democratic forms of government. In the same way, former Communists are struggling to understand what it means to be socialists in a post-Communist world. All religions and ideologies that could once claim singular loyalty, as the sources of sole authority and truth, are coming under assault in the contemporary world. Nearly everyone, nearly everywhere, is experiencing some level of cultural anxiety based on the shift from homogeneous, tight-knit, familial, religiously based communities to heterogeneous, impersonal, detraditionalized societies—or the intermixing of these differing ways of organizing community.

Detraditionalization is not an abstract concept. It has multiple expressions in everyday life. It may be experienced at a local town meeting where residents worry about the change in their community from family farms to exurban development, or at the church meeting where long-time parishioners are arguing with newcomers over the church music program. All Americans experienced the violence wrought by detraditionalization on September 11, 2001, when a group of young Arab men, disoriented and angry over detraditionalization in their homelands (most notably, the importation of American culture and American military presence in Saudi Arabia), enacted their rage against those whom they perceived were responsible for the changes to their "traditional" society.

As with processes of disestablishment, church leaders and congregants feel alarmed by the changes brought on by fragmented and detraditionalized culture. Conflict and violence over these global changes, however, reveal that detraditionalization is not the entire story. Some scholars argue that while many societies have been and are being detraditionalized, traditions have themselves changed and not entirely disappeared. Thus, as a result of detraditionalization, some people are refusing to accept these changes and asserting militant new forms of traditionalism. Even in highly posttraditional cultures, traditions are being relocated, reworked, and sometimes invented anew. As a result, detraditionalization provokes a variety of responses to its challenges to older forms of community—some static and intransigent, some militant and violent, some weary, resigned, or accepting, and perhaps surprisingly, some creative and highly innovative.

Thus, some sociologists argue that while detraditionalization has occurred (and continues to occur), it is happening in tandem with a variety of *retraditioning* processes. "Rather than being envisaged as leading to across-the-board eradication of all traditions," some suggest, detraditionalization "is seen as competing, interpenetrating or interplaying with processes to do with tradition-maintenance, rejuvenation and tradition-construction."[16] According to this coexistence theory, individuals live with both autonomy and "quasi-traditions," making many contemporary lives a "scenario . . . of people having to handle a range of alternatives."[17] Religion is one of the primary ways in which individuals have to navigate and negotiate a "range of alternatives." Clergy and church leaders see the interplay of these forces in both the lives of individual congregants and congregations on a daily—if not hourly—basis.

I agree with Heelas and others who assert that detraditionalization and its attendant retraditioning processes are occurring simultaneously, and I believe this is the context in which individuals and congregations now find themselves. Yet, as part of larger historical movements, it appears that mainline congregations were largely *detraditioned* in the 1960s through the 1980s (Holifield's "participatory congregations" are a detraditionalized form of American Protestantism) and are currently being *retraditioned* through intentionality and in the development of practicing congregations as a new style of congregational organization.

The emergence of new congregational styles suggests that some mainline churches are developing creative and innovative responses to detraditionalization and its pressures. Practicing congregations seem to have accepted some of the wider cultural results of detraditionalization while, at the same time, retraditioning their own communities where Christian faith may be a vital way of life embodied for post-traditional Americans—a generation looking for authentic and purposeful ways to order fragmented and individual existence.

Both disestablishment and detraditionalization are cultural processes. To name them is not an opportunity for assigning blame, as church people often want to do. Rather, to name them and to understand something of their dynamics and history enables congregational leaders to see more clearly the broader pressures and tensions that are causing anxiety in religious communities worldwide. Arguing about tradition, what is traditional, or what should be traditional is no isolated congregational conflict. It is part and parcel of being alive at this moment in human history. It is just the way it is. Much of what is happening in American religious life today is a natural and normal response to living in a time of rapid social transformation. To live in our own time wisely—intentionally, spiritually, and with the eyes of discernment—might be considered one of the most important practices of the Christian life.

Chapter Three

Tradition, Tradition!

Several years ago, I was a member of Grace-St. Luke's Episcopal Church in Memphis, a congregation struggling through a generational conflict regarding change. At the height of the argument, the minister addressed the problems directly one Sunday morning from the pulpit by identifying "the Tevye tension," named after the main character from *Fiddler on the Roof*:

> If you spend any amount of time in the Episcopal Church you will soon discover that there is a tension running through most everything we do . . . Remember Tevye who struggles with tradition on one hand and dealing with progress and changes and growth on the other? It is the struggle between preferring the past [and] facing the future.

Most church fights, he continued, were between hanging onto the past and moving toward the future "by adapting, changing, and growing."[1]

On the morning he preached that sermon, I thought the minister was correct in his assessment of the conflict—two groups, one trying to maintain the way the congregation had always done things; the other, challenging the community to embrace something new. Tradition versus change. The old world versus a new one. Just like *Fiddler on the Roof*. While writing this book, however,

I have thought about that congregation again—mentally revisiting the conflict and thinking through its many dimensions—and have revised my former conclusions. The conflict was not between tradition and change. *The conflict was between rival versions of tradition.* One side had equated tradition with a particular southern way of life, a worldview that had been enshrined in the 1950s under the watch of a particularly powerful clergyman. The other group envisioned its common life around Anglican monasticism, contemplative practices, spiritual direction, and mystical spirituality. They bought a house, christened it "Rivendell" (after the house in *The Lord of the Rings*), and established a daily rule of life for people participating in the community.

Their argument was not about tradition—*everyone* appealed to tradition. Rather, they were arguing over *what tradition* formed the center of congregational identity. A set of traditions created by southern Episcopalians reaching back to nineteenth-century America? Or traditions drawn from the longer history of the Christian church? Both sides had some claim to being the congregation's dominant identity—and they had been struggling with these rival traditions for at least twenty years. Yet they continually cast the argument in terms of tradition versus change instead of seeing the situation as rival traditions, each struggling to adapt to new cultural realities.

To further complicate the picture, each group failed to recognize that its own tradition was changing—neither southern Episcopalianism nor classical Anglican spirituality could be what they once had been. Thus, both sides were simultaneously claiming tradition while changing and adapting it!

The conflict at Grace-St. Luke's illustrates the malleability of tradition. In many, if not most, contemporary arguments no one side can claim sole ownership of tradition—or that they alone are traditionalists. Although clergy and churchgoers rarely consider it, tradition is both necessary for community and is being changed by communities at the same time. As sociologists say, tradition is "invented."[2] French theorist Danièle Hervieu-Léger reminds us, "One has to bear in mind that any tradition develops through the

permanent reprocessing of the data which a group or society re-
ceives from its past."[3] Philosopher Alasdair MacIntyre argues that
"a living tradition then is an historically extended, socially embodied argument, and an argument precisely in part about the
goods which constitute that tradition."[4] Or, as theologian Kathryn
Tanner writes about specifically Christian tradition, it is "the ongoing argument about true discipleship" that constitutes Christian faith.[5] By its very nature, tradition involves imagination,
creativity, ferment, disorder, and conflict. Despite these risks, it is
becoming increasingly clear that a congregation's beliefs, attitudes,
and practices regarding the relationship between tradition and
change are the keys to its vitality.

Varieties of Tradition

If indeed an ongoing argument about the nature of true discipleship is the very definition of tradition, it comes as no surprise that
congregations are constantly struggling over tradition. During
times of rapid social change and cultural dislocations those arguments take on urgency and an increased sense of importance. While
some of the conflicts center on rival traditions, as with Grace-St.
Luke's, others revolve around differing ideas of the very nature of
tradition. Is tradition inviolate, fixed, and unchanging? Or, as suggested in the Grace-St. Luke's story, do traditions necessarily involve adaptation and change?

   For almost two years, I served as the director of adult faith formation at a large congregation in Virginia. One summer, as I
planned for the upcoming Advent, I realized I had a problem: the
church's gift shop, run by the congregation's senior women, held
an annual Christmas sale and party on the first Sunday of Advent
and filled every available educational space with holiday wares and
treats. In order to offer any kind of Advent series, I would have to
ask them to vacate the parish hall in favor of the gym. I approached
Susan Noble (not her real name), the store manager, and explained
the problem.

Mrs. Noble was not happy with my request. The gift shop had been holding its sale since the 1950s and she resisted any suggestion for change. She did not see the need for an Advent series when her gift shop offered such a "nice community Christmas celebration."

I countered by saying that according to the church year Christmas did not even begin until December 25—and it was liturgically and theologically inappropriate to hold a church Christmas party during Advent, a penitential season. And I also explained that younger church-goers were not terribly interested in gift-shop sales. They were seeking spiritual connection with God—something that, for them, happened better through Christian formation than a fundraiser.

Mrs. Noble looked straight in my eyes and said, "Your whole problem is that you don't care about tradition."

I was shocked. After all, I earned a doctorate in church history! Nobody had ever accused me of not caring about tradition. I gazed back with equal firmness and replied, "I do care about tradition. I have a Ph.D. in tradition. But you aren't talking about tradition. You are talking about a custom from the 1950s. The tradition of the church teaches that Advent is a season for prayer, study, and spiritual meditation. Advent is *the* tradition. Not gift-shop sales."

I confess: It was not my most graceful moment as a leader. I did, however, manage to wrest the room from the gift shop's control and offered a successful and well-attended Advent series on peace. But the relationship remained strained. It frustrated me—and it was painful and confusing.

There are many helpful ways to understand this episode—using family-systems theory, conflict management, leadership development, or personality-type analysis. However, I would like to suggest an additional avenue—that of cultural analysis—to explore what happened on that summer afternoon. My argument with Mrs. Noble was a microcosm of tensions felt around the world for the last three centuries. As the speed and reach of social change and innovation have increased, there has been an equal "attempt to structure at least some parts of social life within it as unchanging and invariant."[6] Only after considerable reflection did I understand that Mrs. Noble and I held radically different views of tradition.

Tradition implies repetition, a certain kind of invariability that claims an ancient source: "assumptions, beliefs and patterns of behavior handed down from the past," the Latin *traditio*.[7] However, other concepts are commonly confused—or intertwined—with *traditio*, such as custom, convention, routine, and endowment. In order to understand tradition in relation to congregational vitality, it is important to be able to sort out what people mean when they appeal to tradition.

Custom refers to what people do, actions in accordance with precedent; tradition refers to that which accompanies the action. Customs may (and often must) change, whereas traditions are forms of belief and practice that are understood to have longer historical grounding linked to some more ancient and universal source of authority and meaning. At Mrs. Noble's congregation, the gift-shop sale was a custom. The actions were the customary expression of Christian traditions that are theologically deeper—charity (caring for the poor) and shaping community (creating communal moments of work and play). It may have been possible, if I had been thinking more clearly, to suggest a *new custom* in place of the 1950s Christmas party that would continue the underlying traditions for a new generation of churchgoers.

In addition to conflating custom and tradition, convention and routine are often confused with tradition. Unlike tradition, convention and routine are simply social practices that develop over time—practices with no particular ancient, symbolic, or sacred status. Sociologists define conventions as actions that facilitate practical operations, like raising money for outreach at a church or connecting people to one another in community. Because it is practical and pragmatic, convention and routine should be able to change with changing needs.

Finally, congregations sometimes view tradition as a sort of bank account or endowment—a deposit made long ago—upon which the community draws on a regular basis. In my argument with Mrs. Noble, charity and stable community were, in effect, the principal upon which the gift-shop sale compounded its interest. Many congregations understand tradition in terms of this sort of financial metaphor—tradition is a sacred endowment that they are reluctant to touch, except to increase its holdings. In the treasury model of tradition, congregations often fear engaging traditions lest they diminish them in some way.

Christians often define tradition as fixed, conflating it with ideas of custom, convention, routine, and endowment. In this perspective, tradition must be maintained, guarded, protected, and perpetuated. Such definitions of tradition, however, are becoming increasingly untenable with philosophers and theorists as they recognize that tradition is essentially a dynamic concept, whereby "continuity is capable of incorporating even the innovations and reinterpretations demanded by the present."[8] Sociologist Wade Clark Roof suggests that these two views of tradition are in constant tension in contemporary faith communities. "Religious tradition persists, and will continue to do so," he argues, "but in one of two fundamental ways: either as 'lived tradition,' and thereby in a continual state of reenactment, or hardened into rigid dogmas and moralisms."[9]

In the gift-shop sale quarrel, as with the Grace-St. Luke's argument, both sides appealed to tradition. Thus, it was an argument over rival traditions. An additional level of analysis is important here, however. If the argument were merely about rival traditions, then the issue would be resolved by either congregational preference or which leader had the strongest will or most power. Rival traditions, yes. But rival *definitions* of tradition were at the root of the argument. We were arguing about the very nature of tradition. I was reaching toward a fluid definition of tradition by understanding that it changes over time—and that it is sometimes invented anew. Tradition is "continuously revised and reformulated."[10] In other words, I recognized the dynamic nature of handing down beliefs and practices of the past.

Contemporary social theory recognizes that tradition is "part and parcel of the dynamics of social relations whereby society creates itself" and that it is "not simply a repetition of the past in the present."[11] Rather, the "distinctive mark of tradition is to actualize the past in the present" through communal "re-reading" of rituals, practices, and narratives and "creating a new relationship with the present."[12] In other words, tradition and change function together.

To clarify the complex relationship between tradition and change, French social theorist Georges Balandier distinguished three forms of traditionalism instead of the two responses suggested by Wade Clark Roof. Balandier's three forms of tradition include:

1. *Fundamental traditionalism* "upholds the maintenance of the most deeply rooted values and models of social and cultural observance" and is marked by sense of permanence;
2. *Formal traditionalism* "makes use of forms that are upheld but changed in substance; it establishes a continuity of appearances, but serves new designs"; and
3. *Pseudo-traditionalism* enables a "new construction" of tradition by interpreting the past and assuming continuity while recognizing disorder. It is a stance that calls on the past and, at the same time, "appeases" modernity.[13]

While Balandier is writing for a European audience with distinctive concerns, these three forms of traditionalism translate easily into American congregations. "Fundamental traditionalism" is often nicknamed "fundamentalism" in the United States, a form of religion in which adherents view tradition as fixed "values and models" that must be preserved. Although Americans most readily identify this view of tradition with fundamentalist or evangelical Protestantism, similar impulses of fundamental traditionalism also exist in some branches of Roman Catholicism, Judaism, Hinduism, and Islam. In this mode, people recognize cultural change and reject it in favor of "fixed" tradition—often demonizing their opponents or resorting to violence. Historians tend to identify this form of tradition with so-called "traditional societies," the very kind of social arrangement that is currently deeply embattled and is disappearing under the pressure of cultural fragmentation.

"Formal traditionalism" is the stance adopted toward tradition by much of nineteenth- and twentieth-century mainline Protestantism. Formal traditionalists insist that forms must be maintained while core beliefs may adapt to newer ideas. In mainline denominations this translated into dogged continuity of patterns of ritual, education, roles, and administration while accepting theological changes regarding biblical interpretation, creeds and confessions, sexual ethics, and women in ministry. Thus, many mainline Protestant churches today *appear* exactly the same as (or very similar to) the congregations of a generation ago. However, the substance of teaching and ministry is actually quite different. Formal traditionalists tend to have a difficult time seeing cultural change and accepting its implications in the outward ordering of their lives. In this stance, change is rarely acknowledged and often resisted. Rather, change is acknowledged only when absolutely necessary—changes are made for pragmatic and practical reasons with minimal visible effects. Historically, formal traditionalism is associated with the modern period and reached its zenith around World War II.

The final form, which Balandier calls by the unfortunate name of "pseudo-tradition," echoes Roof's "lived tradition" and is the stance I refer to as *fluid retraditioning*. This view of tradition recognizes the paradoxical nature of modernity and tradition—that modernity creates the possibility for a return to tradition and that tradition "re-reads" and re-creates itself. In this stance, religion is a reconstructed form of tradition within modernity that appeals to a "core lineage" of believing, experiences, and practices based upon the experience of "past witnesses" which emphasizes both continuity and change.[14] People engaged in fluid retraditioning see cultural change, yet unlike the fundamental traditionalists, they accept the demands of change vis-à-vis religious practice as a creative challenge rather than a threat.

Hervieu-Léger refers to this creative rendering of tradition as "a chain of memory," where the "imaginary link with the past and projection into the future are joined."[15] In a sense, fluid retraditioning is the inverse of formal traditionalism, because it willingly innovates with forms (and changes its external appearances) while attempting to return (at some level) to a historic core of practices and beliefs. Some mainline congregations appear to have made—or are making—this move from formal traditionalism to fluid retraditioning.[16]

Thus, Mrs. Noble and I were struggling with tradition on three levels. On the first level, we were arguing over rival traditions. On the second level, we defined tradition differently—she saw it as fixed custom while I understood it as a dynamic historical argument. On the third level, we were functioning out of different paradigms regarding tradition. Neither of us embraced fundamentalist traditionalism. But, having grown up at different times of American history and experiencing mainline Protestantism in entirely different ways, we lived in two different worlds of tradition. We may have both been Episcopalians and been part of the same congregation, but she was a formal traditionalist and I held to Balandier's pseudo-traditionalism (that is, fluid retraditioning). We understood exactly *opposite* things about form and substance, continuity and change.

But what makes this analysis helpful to congregations and religious organizations? Is tradition anything more than an issue of personal preference or congregational taste? Why should clergy and congregational leaders care about sophisticated paradigms regarding tradition as anything other than intellectual play?

There is much more at stake in the argument than is immediately obvious. In a recent article, sociologist Roger Finke suggests that a congregation's stance toward tradition and innovation is foundational to its vitality. He argues that "religious organizations must simultaneously preserve core teaching and generate innovative adaptations" to foster vitality.[17] Drawing off a large body of research, he asserts that mainline Protestantism declined because it did just the opposite of what vital organizations do: Mainline institutions (congregations and denominational structures) changed core traditions while resisting innovation in form.

Although Finke does not refer to Balandier's categories, his analysis implies that the very form of tradition adopted by mainline denominations in the twentieth century (Balandier's "formal traditionalism") caused its loss of spiritual vitality and subsequent membership decline. And, conversely, Finke proposes that preserving "core teaching" linked with innovative forms results in "renewed organizational vitality."[18]

The mistake Finke's article appears to make, however, is to imply that "core teaching" equals conservative theology that must be "preserved" for the overall health and vitality of the organization. A deeper analysis of tradition, however, points out that all core teaching changes over time. Thus, it cannot be simply preserved. Even in groups that believe they are preserving tradition, ironic (and often unnoticed) adaptations and adjustments occur. Core teaching can remain central, part of the longer tradition while it is being re-read, reconstructed, or reappropriated; and core teaching might include a variety of beliefs, interpretations, and practices that actually change over time.

Thus, core teaching should not be misconstrued as a simple return to a literal reading of the Bible or Christian creeds. In mainline congregations core teaching might include the practice of reading the Bible through critical methods or returning to scripture study by employing new tools of narrative theology. The core teaching of mainline Protestantism, the tradition itself, involves a certain degree of dynamism and change—the reformed church always reforming. Finke's article appears to grant core teaching an immutable status that is, according to other sociologists and historians, a myth. Thus, for mainline Protestants, core teaching might be better defined as Hervieu-Léger's "chain of memory," the imaginative and creative link between past, present, and future.

Although Finke misses some nuances of mainline Protestantism, his essential point about tradition and innovation as central to vitality is well taken—especially when interwoven with more finely tuned definitions of tradition. Mainline congregations that understand the dynamic relationship between tradition and innovation, between continuity and change, between the past and the present, those that identify themselves as part of a lived "chain of memory," are vital communities in which the past becomes part of meaning-making for people striving to make sense of their existence. Without the chain of memory, congregations become institutional amnesiacs, lost without identity or vocation. Of necessity, they will lose both members and vitality. What is needed is the "innovative return," as Finke puts it, to tradition.

Theology of Tradition

Seeing tradition as malleable and fluid is not, however, an invention of philosophers, social critics, and sociologists. The dynamism of tradition is, in itself, part of Jewish and Christian tradition! Tensions and paradoxes of tradition and change can be found throughout the Hebrew and Christian scriptures. Things prohibited by one part of scripture are practiced by other believers at a later time. Over the centuries recorded in the Bible, Jewish practice adapts to a variety of historical pressures.

In the New Testament, Christians adjusted Jewish practice to their own ends. Entire books can be construed as elaborate arguments over tradition as Jesus' followers retained, re-read, reinterpreted, and reappropriated their Jewish chain of memory. Every week, Christians participate in the Eucharist or Lord's Supper, which is one of the most dramatic examples of appropriating an old tradition—the Jewish Passover—by inventing a new tradition. Perhaps the greatest change in scriptural tradition is the understanding of God—from hints of polytheism to a strict monotheism and, eventually, to the philosophically sophisticated idea of trinitarianism (a concept that reaches its fullest development outside the pages of scripture).

Many Christians have struggled with how the nature and practice of their faith has changed over the centuries. Cardinal John Henry Newman, who wrestled with the dynamic nature of Christian tradition, put the case quite clearly:

If Christianity be a universal religion, suited not simply to one locality or period, but to all times and all places, it cannot but vary in its relations and dealings towards the world around it, that is, it will develop. Principles require a very various application according as persons and circumstances vary, and must be thrown into new shapes according to the form of society which they are to influence. Hence all bodies of Christians, orthodox or not, develop the doctrines of Scripture.[19]

For Newman, the fullness of faith rested only in the mind of God; human expression of Christianity would—of necessity—grow and change over time until it reached "full elucidation" of truth.

Although Newman's nineteenth-century optimism over the progress of human tradition now seems dated, he correctly analyzed a modern problem. Unlike Christians in centuries past, thoughtful believers recognize the dizzying variation of tradition in time and through cultures. The very act of passing something down through time changes the thing itself. Tradition always changes. And, at its heart, Christianity is dynamic tradition.

And it is also, in many cases, invented tradition. One sociologist defines tradition invention as follows: "*Invented tradition* is taken to mean a set of practices, normally governed by overtly or tacitly accepted rules and of a ritual or symbolic nature, which seek to inculcate certain values and norms of behavior by repetition, which automatically implies continuity with the past."[20] Striking examples of invented tradition include the so-called "ancient" rituals of the British monarchy (such as Prince Charles' installation as the Prince of Wales), the Boy Scouts, the symbol of Uncle Sam, Scottish Highland games, Santa Claus, and Christmas. All claimed to be traditions from antiquity. Yet each is a modern development (within the last two centuries)—created at specific points in time for specific cultural purposes.

From tabernacle to Temple, and synagogue to basilica, ancient Hebrews and early Christians invented traditions. Throughout the long centuries of church history, Christians continued to invent tradition, too. There are many obvious examples—such as monastic reform movements, Martin Luther and the birth of Protestantism, and the Wesleyan revival. However, there are less obvious examples as well. In the nineteenth century, Christians constructed elaborate neo-Gothic church buildings, dressed clergy in monastic-type garb, and recreated or rejuvenated medieval spiritual practices. The architecture, liturgy, or disciplines they borrowed bore little relation to medieval Christian faith as medieval people experienced it. Victorian romanticism posited mystery and transcendence in Christian practice against an increasingly technical, mechanistic, and scientific existence in modern cities. By inventing medieval traditions anew, nineteenth-century people found communal expression of their own romantic ideals of faith—which helped them cope with the changes of a confusing present.

Tradition changes over time—sometimes as a calculated strategy and other times as an ad hoc sort of popular response to social circumstances. Although traditions are always changing, being created and recreated, historians suspect that tradition invention occurs "more frequently when a rapid transformation of society weakens or destroys the social patterns for which 'old' traditions had been designed . . . and their institutional carriers and promulgators no longer prove sufficiently adaptable and flexible."[21] For their entire history, Christians have invented, recreated, or adapted traditions when old patterns no longer hold sway. Thus, fluid retraditioning is an expression of the theological imagination, as biblical tradition is lived out in community, and is an ancient practice of faith that connects Christians to their ancestors.

Retraditioning as a Congregational Practice

In October 2000, an article in the *Wall Street Journal* caught my attention: "Protestants Look to Their Roots: After Decades of Ecumenism, Denominations Emphasize Sectarian Brand Identity." The article reported on several mainline denominations that are developing both publicity and adult formation materials to be more intentional about teaching their history and distinctive practices.

One of the unique characteristics of American Protestantism in the post-World War II period was the decline of loyalty to "brand name" denominations. For several decades, congregations and denominational mission boards muted their traditional identity in favor of generic versions of Christian belief and worship to better serve a "post-denominational age." Yet now, according to the *Wall Street Journal* story, some denominations are reengaging tradition as a way of increasing member commitment and recruiting new members.

While at least one sociologist identified this shift as a top-down church growth strategy, I have experienced this intentional return to tradition from exactly the opposite direction—in several congregations from the pews up! Indeed, many American congregations have found success in being post-traditional or postdenominational, but it also appears that some are finding new vitality through a new emphasis on tradition and history. In both my research and my own church attendance, I have noted younger church members are attracted to particular congregations because those churches are clear about their tradition.[22] The *Wall Street Journal* was reporting one of the most under-reported religion stories in the country—the retraditioning of mainline Protestantism.

Twentieth-century American Protestants grew up in mainline churches whose characteristics were largely constructed in the age of the social congregation, from 1870 to 1950. The ideals of birthright denominationalism—of God as an authority figure, ministry as the actions of paid male professionals, of the church as a social "home" with the parish hall as its center, and of the congregation as a religious civic organization that served both God and country—wove a Protestant cloth of identity that was, in the minds of many churchgoers, *the* Christian faith. These customs spoke to a particular experience of American history—and the practices and institutions they created worked in that context. And these patterns formed what is called "establishment Protestantism."

But those particular patterns—characteristics some people still associate with the meaning of faith—are no longer "sufficiently adaptable and flexible" for the purposes they were constructed. Those nineteenth- and twentieth-century patterns are the precise patterns that have been "detraditioned" in America's newer multivocal culture.

Much of the recent history of American Protestantism can be understood as a quest to retradition in relation to the changes. As the old Protestant culture was disestablished and detraditioned, local congregations responded in a variety of ways. Some simply accepted the conclusions of cultural change and self-defined as "nondenominational" or "post-traditional," most naturally aligning themselves with evangelical or charismatic religion. Others attempted to maintain inviolate traditions—often taking the form of religious fundamentalism or rigid resistance to change. In more recent years, some have attempted to rejuvenate tradition in a variety of ways. And still other congregations now appear to be constructing new traditions.

In the conflict over the gift-shop sale, Mrs. Noble was resisting cultural change through tradition maintenance—as were the congregants at Grace-St. Luke's who were upholding the virtues of southern Episcopalianism. Not theological fundamentalists, they nevertheless had codified an orthodoxy of convention that needed to be guarded at all costs. In theologically moderate to liberal mainline congregations, tradition maintenance is probably the most common strategy employed by congregations anxious about the larger results of cultural fragmentation. And it is in answer to the problems raised by a tradition-maintenance mode that the diagnostic style of congregational vitality developed.

Tradition maintenance is not the only form of retraditioning, however. In the gift-shop argument, I adopted the posture of fluid retraditioning when I tried to rejuvenate tradition by reintroducing a largely secularized Protestant congregation to the spiritual rhythms of the Christian year. In essence, I was reaching back past the conventions of established Protestantism toward more ancient patterns of Christian practice and attempting to enliven the congregation through renewed appreciation of a historic tradition.

At Grace-St. Luke's, some congregants were reconstructing tradition. Borrowing ideas and cultural materials from the past (living in Christian community, practicing hourly prayer), they stitched together a contemporary rendering of ancient practice—thus "inventing" the Rivendell community. They both adapted tradition and invented it. In the conflict at Grace-St. Luke's, both sides felt pressured living in a fractured culture. Yet, they responded in different ways: one maintaining local and recent tradition, the other constructing new traditions from older sources. In the process, these rival traditions competed for the soul of the congregation. Retraditioning is a simpler concept than its awkward name implies. It is a process wherein individuals—and congregations—are responding to the larger cultural results of modern fragmentation by creating communities that provide sacred space for the formation of identity and meaning, the construction of "pockets" of connectedness to the long history of Christian witness and practice in a disconnected world. As one cultural theorist summarizes it, "Everything seems to conspire these days against distant goals, lifelong projects, lasting commitments, eternal alliances, immutable identities."[23] Accordingly, life is random, contingent, and fractured.

Some congregations seem to understand innately that their basic task in this kind of culture is to resist contemporary fragmentation, contingency, and autonomy by embodying robust traditions that connect people to God, each other, the past, and a hopeful future, regardless of what specific form that takes. Yet, in its fixed forms, retraditioning translates into religious fundamentalism, sectarian isolationism, or resistance to all forms of change. When fixed definitions of tradition are the norm, a congregation's primary orientation will be protection, guardianship, and maintenance.

In its more fluid forms of rejuvenation, adaptation, and invention, retraditioning implies reaching back to the past, identifying practices that were an important part of that past, and bringing them to the present where they can reshape contemporary life. In this mode, congregations will tend toward reflexivity (willingness to change through engagement with tradition and an equal willingness to change the tradition through engagement), reflection (thoughtfulness about practice and belief), and risk taking.

Bearing Tradition

Tradition cannot be engaged alone. Participation in tradition is always communal. As institutions become detraditionalized, and the general culture is less communal, there are fewer and fewer places where history and tradition can be located. As Danièle Hervieu-Léger points out, "One of the chief characteristics of modern societies is that they are no longer societies of memory."[24] Contemporary culture suffers from collective amnesia. Religious communities, specifically congregations, are one place where individuals hope to connect with larger communal, moral, and spiritual traditions. But sadly, some mainline Protestant congregations have fallen victim to the larger cultural amnesia by forgetting who— and whose—they are.

Indeed, if the *very definition* of religion is a "chain of memory," the practice of *anamnesis,* the "recalling to memory of the past," must be central to congregational life.[25] Insofar as congregations understand themselves as living communities in a lineage of witnesses, their work entails redefining and adapting tradition that they have receive and must pass on. As a British sociologist comments, "Community, whatever our understanding, in order to be community must have duration and thus must necessarily entail some notion of tradition."[26] But the communal nature of tradition raises a question: What notions of tradition can *enliven* contemporary congregations instead of consigning churches to the cultural role of religious antiquarians?

Theologian Dorothy Bass explores the tension of tradition in congregations by noting that

> Congregations have stood at the crossroads of conservation and change in American religion, facing back to a cherished inheritance and forward through the contexts of the contemporary lives. And at this crossroads, a characteristic tension prevails . . . This tension inheres in each congregation's dual nature as a local, culturally enmeshed entity and as the member, nonetheless, of a great transnational tradition.[27]

In this tension, Bass insists that all congregations embody the "ongoing argument" of Christian discipleship as both bearers and shapers of tradition. Continuity and change.

But not all congregations participate in this process in conscious ways which leads, Bass implies, to flattened notions of tradition that fail to foster vitality. She claims that "not only do congregations rely upon traditions, but traditions rely upon them."[28] She thus places congregations in the center of a reflexive cultural task of fluid retraditioning—urging Christians to see themselves not only as "receivers" of tradition but as *makers* of future tradition. Such a vocation cannot help but inculcate corporate vision and vitality as congregations intentionally participate in both claiming the past and creating a better future. In this work, both memory and imagination are nurtured and exercised by clergy and the baptized in community.

Sociologists Wade Clark Roof and Jackson Carroll build on this idea to suggest possible new paths for mainline Protestant revitalization. Borrowing the notion that congregations are bearers of tradition, they argue that denominations themselves are "communities of memory."

> They are communities that affirm, preserve, and transmit a distinctive sense of who they are. This identity is rooted in a cultural narrative, or set of meanings, shaped by historical and social experience. Memory draws upon values, symbols, and traditions that reach far into the past.

In a "post-Protestant age," mainline denominations need to "re-symbolize the tradition to address new circumstances."[29]

Practicing congregations, such as Church of the Epiphany in Washington, appear to be doing exactly what Roof and Carroll state is necessary for revitalizing mainline Protestantism—heightening the sense of "religious consciousness" while, at the same time, cultivating a more demanding sense of membership as "re-symbolized" by adapting Christian tradition through meaningful practices.[30]

Key to fluid retraditioning is the idea of memory, of passing on the faith, as Bass, Roof, and Carroll point out. Christian communities can no longer assume that congregants know their story; it must be imaginatively told, retold, and enacted, so that tradition becomes a living thing. Practicing congregations are dynamic learning communities in which this process occurs. These churches model a particular way of life; communities of practice that forge, express, and bear certain traditions.[31] Thus, these congregations both carry and craft tradition in intentional ways—"fluid retraditioning"—while the surrounding culture has disconnected itself from the moorings of a (mostly) Protestant past in a detraditioned world. All congregations bear tradition. But practicing congregations both bear traditions and transform them at the same time—they are reflexive communities. Whereas establishment-style mainline churches viewed tradition as fixed, practicing congregations see tradition as dynamic, fluid, and lived reality.

Intermingling in Congregations

Developing my own understanding of tradition and the forms of tradition in congregations has helped me see dynamics in faith communities that are often invisible. At Grace-St. Luke's, for example, both sides of the quarrel probably would have agreed that their congregation should bear tradition. However, only one group would have thought it appropriate to reshape tradition intentionally in the process. The questions in that conflict were layered, involving both tradition rivalry and fundamental definitions of tradition: Which tradition? How do you pass tradition on? What is the relationship between tradition and change? But it was hard to see the questions in the midst of division.

At the other church, Mrs. Noble wanted to guard a fixed tradition. I thought a "new" ancient tradition—careful attention to the church year—needed to replace the customary gift-shop sale. She interpreted my (rather ungraceful) desire to change tradition as an attack on her and what she understood as the Christian way of life. Unlike Grace-St. Luke's, where arguing over tradition sparked a congregation-wide conflict, Mrs. Noble and I had a leadership quarrel over what constituted tradition that resulted in little more than bruised feelings. Neither of us realized that we were arguing about the "chain of memory" that was foundational to the congregation's future vitality.

Both examples—Grace-St. Luke's and Mrs. Noble—highlight a final aspect of thinking about tradition in congregations: conflict. Historians and sociologists have long noted that in the "boundary areas" where rival traditions "intermingle," conflict is the likely result. This is most obvious with immigrant communities—especially in cities where multiple immigrant traditions live side by side. In geographic boundaries between Vietnamese, Sudanese, and Salvadoran communities (including multiple internal tribal boundaries), high levels of crime and gang violence are commonplace. In such locales not only do rival traditions conflict, but different generations within the same tradition also argue about the nature of tradition and how it should be practiced in a new setting. When traditions are uprooted and remoored, tension and conflict between traditions and cross-generations are inevitable.[32]

Grace-St. Luke's and Mrs. Noble are examples of both conflict between traditions and cross-generational conflict about tradition. In essence, they illustrate that in contemporary American society, congregations function as "immigrant" communities, where traditions intermingle as religious "aliens" try to embody Christian discipleship in a larger, detraditionalized culture. Local traditions are being uprooted; younger generations are challenging old patterns and trying to remoor the congregation to different traditions. Communal and personal conflict are the result.

But conflict is not the only story of immigrant communities. As sociologist John Thompson rightly points out, "it should also be stressed that this process of intermingling is also a source of enormous cultural creativity and dynamism." He continues:

> [Intermingling] creates a kind of cultural restlessness which is
> constantly shifting directions, assuming new forms and depart-
> ing from established conventions in unexpected ways. And it

attests to the fact that, in a world increasingly traversed by cultural migrations and communication flows, traditions are less sheltered than ever before from the potentially invigorating consequences of encounters with the other.[33]

This is profoundly good news for mainline congregations where intermingling and argument over tradition occur on a daily—if not hourly—basis. At this moment in American history, congregations can be seen as "culturally restless" places, where, if leaders are wise, "new forms" of tradition can arise. Conflicts over tradition are probably not best seen as problems to be fixed. Rather, conflict—that "ongoing argument"—is the very heart of Christian tradition, the stuff from which Christian faith is made—and remade. And because the conflicts are so evident, the lively reality of almost all congregations, it is a sign of the creative and "potentially invigorating" work of God's Spirit among us.

But conflict alone does not automatically translate into vitality. Without wise spiritual leadership, it can manifest itself in abuse, division, and violence. Thus, the "ongoing argument" needs to be reframed as the creative intermingling of traditions—something that happens as traditions are embodied in the intentional practices of faith, when a way of life is remembered and shared in Christian community.

Chapter Four

Practice Makes Pilgrims

I do not think I could ever forget the first time I read Dietrich Bonhoeffer. When I was a college student in the late 1970s both *The Cost of Discipleship* and *Life Together* were assigned in religious studies courses. Bonhoeffer's call to reject "cheap grace" and embrace a way of costly discipleship resonated with my own youthful hopes for authentic Christian living—and his description of the semi-monastic Protestant community at Finkenwalde stirred my longings to be part of a vibrant and vital Christian community. Over the years, many books have passed through my library, but those two, the inexpensive paperback editions bearing the idealistic comments and enthusiastic markings of a teenage theologian, remain on my bookshelf.

Occasionally, I return to Bonhoeffer to reclaim the vision to which he opened my young eyes:

> Cheap grace is the preaching of forgiveness without requiring repentance, baptism without church discipline, Communion without confession, absolution without personal confession. Cheap grace is grace without discipleship, grace without the cross, grace without Jesus Christ, living and incarnate.[1]

In *The Cost of Discipleship*, Bonhoeffer attacks Christianity that is based on rationality and intellectual assent, legalism and pietism, in favor of faith that is a robust way of life in community, using language that seemed to describe the mainline congregation to which I had been born. "The world of cheap grace," he insisted, "has been the ruin of more Christians than any commandment of works."[2] To Bonhoeffer, and to paraphrase the writer of James, beliefs without practices were dead. In *Life Together,* he again attacked cheap grace by describing the particular Christian practices that frame such a way of life in community—daily worship, confession, care, study, prophetic witness, and hospitality.

As I look back at Dietrich Bonhoeffer's words, I realize that as a young adult I wanted authentic Christianity, coherence of message and practice, and the transforming power of God in community. And, over the years, I have been surprised at how many people I know who were similarly affected by Bonhoeffer's vision. As it happened, those longings were not the isolated desires of an individual but an expression of a larger cultural hunger in which many people were seeking a meaningful way of life. Some of my peers became perpetual seekers; others wound up as evangelical, or "born again," Christians (and sometimes even fundamentalists). But some stayed around mainline congregations, eventually to become clergy, leaders, and theologians in those communities. (And still others, like me, blended these options: I was born into mainline religion, journeyed with fundamentalists, evangelicals, and charismatics for a time, and returned home to mainline church as an adult.) In turn, that corporate longing for meaningful Christian discipleship is pressing institutional Protestantism to reform itself in ways suggested by Dietrich Bonhoeffer and has led to an increased emphasis on Christian practices.

"There is in the Christian churches," writes Craig Dykstra, "and in the United States as a whole, a profound spiritual hunger for something . . . [people] yearn for coherent, thoughtful guidance as well as fresh access to the deep veins of wisdom that at least some of them suspect are still there to be mined from historic religious traditions."[3] Theologian Jonathan Wilson argues that only "faithful communities" that embody a "new monasticism" by "practicing church" can give Christians a framework for living their lives and overcome the moral fragmentation of the contemporary world.[4]

New monasticism? Christian practices? These are no longer theoretical constructs or visionary longings. Rather, these desires are becoming realities in the lives of Christian believers and in their communities. New Testament scholar Marcus Borg has observed this as well: "[A]n encouraging sign of renewal in the church in North America is the recovery of practice as central to the Christian life."[5] Although it can sometimes be difficult to see, a new kind of mainline congregation is being rebirthed around Christian practices.

Congregational Monasticism

Zygmunt Bauman, a British theorist of postmodernism, claims that "one can think of postmodern life as one lived in a city in which traffic is daily re-routed and street names are liable to be changed without notice. . . . In such a city one is well advised not to plan long and time consuming journeys. The shorter the trip, the greater the chance of completing it." Accordingly, contingency and fragmentation shape the world we now inhabit, whose form is, by nature, flexible and malleable. "To be rational in the *modern* world," he further states, "meant to be a pilgrim and to live one's life as a pilgrimage. To be rational in the *postmodern* world means to be a vagrant or a tourist, or to act as one."[6]

There is much to support Bauman's claims. Many (if not most) contemporary people live as vagrants—spiritually, intellectually, geographically, morally, and relationally. From the perspectives of traditional faith communities, these are discomforting observations. Vague awareness of this new reality creates much social anxiety and can potentially fuel fundamentalisms, inquisitions, and culture wars.

Listen, however, to the contrasting testimony of writer Nora Gallagher about her congregation, Trinity Episcopal Church in Santa Barbara, California: "I came to this church five years ago as a tourist and ended up as a pilgrim."[7] Trinity is a theologically progressive church that embodies faith through a variety of renewed Christian practices. Through the rhythms of the Christian calendar, a year of participating in a community's faith practices,

Gallagher sharpened and deepened her sense of identity in God and discerned the Spirit's call to love and service. Unlike the tourist, she decided to stay and put down roots—not participating in church as some sort of spiritual thrill seeking, but choosing instead to learn the community's native language and its "routine quotidianity," that is, its everyday practices of faith.[8] She ceased moving through space in which others dwell; instead, she inhabited ancient Christian space by adopting its time, its seasons, its ethics, and its patterns. In a palpable way, she learned to participate in a reality expressed by the earliest Christian communities: "But you are a chosen family, a royal priesthood, a holy nation, a people to be God's private property, so that you may announce the virtues of the One who called you out of darkness into his marvelous light" (1 Peter 2:9).

Gallagher's experience is profoundly suggestive for contemporary congregations. In an age of fragmentation, it may well be the case that the vocation of congregations is to turn tourists into pilgrims—those who no longer journey aimlessly, but, rather, those who journey in God and whose lives are mapped by the grace of Christian practices. But what did Gallagher find at Trinity Episcopal Church that compelled her to cease spiritual vacationing and embark on Christian pilgrimage against the postmodern tide?

Indeed, Gallagher discovered something counterintuitive at Trinity, something perhaps even a bit nonrational—that the ideal of the Christian congregation as a pilgrim community provides powerful moral and spiritual ballast in a radically fragmented world. The "rational" postmodern choice may be, as Bauman asserts, spiritual tourism—life without a map, without destination. But Christian congregations do not exist to provide rational choices. They exist as an alternative sort of logic that offers hospitality to strangers and wayfarers and forms people in an ancient way of being in God. As a by-product, such congregations challenge the "rationalities" of postmodern life by crafting distinctly Christian ways of life. Congregations provide a way of exploring moral, religious, communal, and personal identity that moves with purpose and intention through the ever-shifting terrain of the postmodern city.

Although Nora Gallagher's experience seems quintessentially postmodern, it is not historically unique. Ancient and medieval church history is rife with accounts of vagrants and tourists, mostly people uprooted by social turmoil and war, who find their way to monasteries for temporary shelter or safety and wind up as novices, later to become brothers and sisters. In such accounts, the spiritual vagrant is transfixed by the way of life practiced behind the monastery walls—the life where time is marked by prayer, hospitality, study, and communal care. Through intentional and habitual practices, daily spirituality, life traced both meaning and holiness in a chaotic world.

The odd thing about Nora Gallagher's tale is not that she found a Christian way of life in community—something so compelling that she joined their pilgrimage. Men and women have been doing that for centuries. The odd thing is that Gallagher found it in a *mainline* Protestant congregation in the 1990s! Only a few years before her arrival, Trinity was suffering from the usual set of mainline woes: declining membership, a decaying urban building, conflict, little vision, and poor leadership. Through a series of unexpected events, the congregation was able to reinvent itself as a kind of *open* monastic community—a place of spiritual practices, hospitality, worship, and justice.[9]

In their essay "Christian Practices and Congregational Education in Faith," Craig Dykstra and Dorothy Bass suggest that congregations are like monastic communities with "porous" borders that present faith as a "way of life" instead of a Christian "life style." Drawing a distinction between the practices "of the world" and the practices of the Christian community, Dykstra and Bass assert that "congregations are the setting where people look for the resources to bridge these contexts—the places where they hope to learn about life-giving patterns of life suited to the multiple complex contexts in which they now live."[10]

Through most of American history, mainline Protestant congregations did not conceive of themselves as monastic communities with porous boundaries! More often, at least in the Protestant mainline into which I was born, congregations were the religious equivalent of Rotary or the Chamber of Commerce, a kind of family club that you attended on Sunday morning. The congregations of my youth had Christian practices. Those practices tended to be implicit and assumed, a kind of accident of birth. And Christian practices were also blurred. That is, they took on the "practices of the world" with little or no theological reflection. Thus, for much of the twentieth century (if not longer) the Protestant mainline had flattened Christian practices through both lack of attention to such holy habits and by depending upon the surrounding culture to teach and support a Christian way of life.

Although Dykstra and Bass seem to imply that all congregations are like monastic communities with porous boundaries, it is evident that some congregations have become more intentional about the monastic quality of their communities in recent years. In paying such attention, congregations are finding new senses of vitality. Trinity in Santa Barbara is one such example. But there are many others. In Yorktown, Virginia, members of St. Mark Evangelical Lutheran Church participate in a way of prayer and discernment based on the St. Ignatian retreat. At Calvin Presbyterian in Zelienople, Pennsylvania, congregants engage spiritual practices in the context of governance. In Naples, Florida, Cornerstone United Methodist Church introduces new members to the semi-monastic practices of John Wesley and early British Methodism. St. George's Episcopal Church in Arlington, Virginia took classical Christian practices to the heart of its renewed sense of identity as an "urban abbey" that includes a congregational "rule of life."

These churches' clarity may be unique, but renewed appreciation of monastic practice in the mainline is not. Books like Kathleen Norris's *The Cloister Walk* and Phyllis Tickle's daily prayer manuals are bestsellers among mainline Protestants. Literally scores of mainline congregations now sponsor everything from studies on Benedictine spirituality to Celtic daily prayer and thirty-day Ignatian retreats. Year-long catechesis processes in some Lutheran, Episcopal, Methodist, and Presbyterian congregations demonstrate a similar spiritual seriousness by forming new members as though they were novices. And *real* monasteries book retreatants far in advance because so many people want to participate in their common life.

Although there may be some level of "what's hot" in spiritual consumerism happening here, I believe that all these things express a deeper hunger for meaningful Christian faith. It is possible to offer trendy programming in spirituality, as if the congregation were a kind of religious shopping mall or boutique. Not all practices can form pilgrim congregations. When congregations pay attention to Christianity and its constituent practices *as a way of life*, only then are they acting as open monastic communities. As was true in earlier centuries of Christianity, communal practices have the power of turning tourists into pilgrims.

Theologian Jonathan Wilson writes on the "new monasticism," a reordering of Christian community necessary to embody the virtues of faith in a postmodern world. Wilson builds his argument off of a suggestion from philosopher Alasdair MacIntyre. At the end of his *After Virtue*, MacIntyre writes:

> What matters at this stage [of history] is the construction of local forms of community within which civility and the intellectual and moral life can be sustained through the new dark ages which are already upon us. And if the tradition of the virtues was able to survive the horrors of the last dark ages, we are not entirely without grounds for hope. This time however the barbarians are not waiting beyond the frontiers; they have already been governing us for quite some time. And it is our lack of consciousness of this that constitutes part of our predicament. We are waiting not for a Godot, but for another—doubtless very different—St. Benedict.[11]

Wilson, however, is not just *waiting* for St. Benedict. Rather, he calls for "Christian communities that may produce a new St. Benedict." As an Anabaptist, he primarily argues for a separatist or withdrawal strategy for this new monasticism and offers several potential forms that such intentional community might take.[12] Gallagher, Dykstra, and Bass point to the tantalizing possibility that some sort of new monasticism might already exist—or could potentially exist—within the context of mainline Protestant churches as congregation-based, grassroots responses to postmodern culture through a renewal of theological imagination and Christian practices.[13]

When I was a college student reading Bonhoeffer, *Life Together* appealed to me because it described a Christian community practicing faith together "where it understands itself as being part of the one, holy, catholic, Christian church, where it shares actively and passively in the sufferings and struggles and promise of the whole Church."[14] When I first read Bonhoeffer, I was attending an evangelical college and worshiping at evangelical churches. Evangelicalism had practices galore, but it lacked any sense of connection to the historic church or Christian traditions outside its own particular subculture. Bonhoeffer's ecumenical vision is linked to what theologian L. Gregory Jones identifies as "the centrality of disciplines and practices for Christian life."[15] The community Bonhoeffer described was both spiritually serious *and* ecclesial.

An American commonplace separates spirituality and church: One must be either "spiritual" or "religious." But Bonhoeffer's vision—and indeed the long thread of Benedictine practice—refuses to separate spirituality from the context of the church and its local expression in congregations. Thus, the unique combination of historic Protestant ecumenism and Christian practice might well be a fertile seedbed for mainline vitality in new congregational forms of Dykstra and Bass's "porous monasticism." And it was such a combination that drew Nora Gallagher from the wanderings of a tourist into a life of Christian pilgrimage.

Practices: A Way of Life

If such congregations are emerging, they are being formed around clusters of Christian practices—not out of any denominational program or church-growth strategy. Rather, these communities are reflecting deep cultural changes in American spirituality as they respond to (and, in turn, shape) experiences and longings of their clergy, congregants, and newcomers. In the late 1990s, Princeton sociologist Robert Wuthnow suggested that American religion was undergoing a shift from seeker spirituality to practice-oriented spirituality.[16] "To say that spirituality is practiced," Wuthnow writes, "means that people engage intentionally in activities that deepen their relations to the sacred. . . . Broadly conceived, spiritual practice is a cluster of intentional activities concerned with relating to the sacred."[17]

In recent years, theologians, ethicists, and religious studies scholars have explored the terrain of religious practice, attempting to clarify the term. According to Dorothy Bass, "Practices are those shared activities that address fundamental human needs and that, woven together, form a way of life."[18] Historian David Hall recognizes the complexity of the term and defines "practice" as "culture in action" that "encompasses the tension, the ongoing struggle of definition, [and which is] constituted within every religious tradition and [that is] always present in how people choose to act."[19] Likewise, historian Colleen McDannell claims, "All religious practices convey knowledge through action . . . Religious practice is more than merely lived. Religious practice is also *imagined.*"[20] Theologian Craig Dykstra writes that "practices are those cooperative human activities through which we, as individuals and communities, grow and develop in moral character and substance."[21] And New Testament scholar Marcus Borg says simply, "Practice is about living of the Christian way."[22]

From this mosaic of definitions, we can begin to see the larger picture of practice. Christian practices are both individual and corporate. Christian practices embody belief, and, conversely, beliefs form practices. Christian practices are the constituent parts of a larger Christian way of life, as revealed, modeled, and taught by Jesus Christ. Christian practices necessarily involve reflection, imagination, tension, attention, and intentionality. Practices imply practice, repetition, craft, habit, and art. Christians engage these actions for their own sake—because they are good and worthy and beautiful—not because they are instruments to some other end (like increasing membership or marketing the congregation). Practices possess standards of maturity and excellence to which practitioners can aspire.

Practices fall roughly into three definitional categories: moral, ascetical, and anthropological. Moral practices—activities like hospitality, healing, dying well, stewardship, doing justice, and caring—stress communal formation in virtue. Ascetical practices, including contemplation, silence, and union with God—things that may be achieved by a variety of means in the form of spiritual exercises—emphasize deep connection with God and personal Christian maturity. An anthropological approach to practice resists fixing such actions. Rather, Christian practices are just the things that Christian people do—"eating, meeting, and greeting"— as they negotiate their faith in relation to the larger culture; theological reflection arises within "the ordinary workings of Christian lives."[23] Whatever the differences between these approaches, they all integrate faith and life, define practices as social and historical, understand that practices are part of living tradition, and articulate a kind of theological wisdom embodied in the life of all God's people.[24]

When Christians understand that what they do comprises a way of life that is corporate, ancient, and wise, the theological imagination opens wide. Prayer is more than an isolated personal exercise. Rather, depending on the kind of prayer, the practitioner may be participating in a practice of contemplation, study, discernment, healing, doing justice, or friendship. Making coffee for the welcome hour is more than a task; it is a constituent piece of hospitality, a small action that allows for the practice of welcoming the stranger to take place. From the perspective of practice, worship is not a matter of congregational taste. Rather, it expresses in liturgical form all the practices a community cherishes—singing, intercession, connection with God, contemplation, study, formation in faith, and hospitality. Through worship, you can "see" nearly all the practices of a congregation expressed in its art, music, architecture, word, and symbolic action.

Christian practices are all these things—the things Bonhoeffer wrote about in *Life Together*; the things St. Benedict outlined in his *Rule*. In an Advent sermon about the wilderness, Nora Gallagher preached, "Where must we go, *where* is the place we are called that has no maps, and different guides."[25] Postmodern people live in that *where*—the city with no maps. Yet those "different guides," practices of faith, can point the way to God and love. Practice might not make perfect, but it does appear to make pilgrims.

The Practicing Mainline?

One of the lesser-noted findings of the Hartford Institute for Religious Research's massive Faith Communities Today (FACT) study was the link between "personal spiritual practices" and congregational vitality. According to study codirector David Roozen, "The study does confirm that the more emphasis a congregation gives to the values of home and personal religious practices the higher the congregation's vitality and the more likely it is to be growing in membership."[26] According to their data, "oldline Protestants" placed least emphasis on spiritual practices, family devotions, and Sabbath keeping than any other religious grouping (compared with evangelical Protestants, Roman Catholics, and Eastern Orthodox) and showed corresponding low vitality. "In fact," Roozen argues, "the lack of emphasis on . . . practices appears to be one of the reasons that, overall, oldline congregations are less 'vital' and less likely to be growing than evangelical Protestant congregations."[27]

The link proved compelling enough that Roozen ran a statistical simulation to answer the question, "What if oldline Protestant congregations emphasized personal spiritual practices as much as evangelical Protestant congregations?" In the simulation, mainline congregations that were intentional about Christian practices showed a marked increase in both vitality and numerical growth—nearly catching up to vitality and growth rates in evangelical Protestant congregations.

Interestingly enough, the study did note that mainline congregations emphasizing spiritual practices were also more likely to be growing than other mainline churches. This does not mean, of course, that the "new monasticism" is sweeping through American religion. It does mean, however, that a new interest in practices is finding its way even into America's oldest congregations, churches that have been struggling for decades. And closer attention to practice, by its very nature, is yet another factor contributing to the development of a new style of mainline congregation —a discerning congregation that both practices what it preaches and preaches practices.

	Moral (Bass & Dykstra)	Ascetical (Coakley)	Anthropological (Tanner)
What it means by "practice"	"A cluster of activities, ideas, and images, lived by Christian people over time, which addresses a fundamental human need in the light of and in response to God's active presence for the life of the world in Jesus Christ." Practices are done for their own sake.	Disciplines that shape the self and deepen over time by grace through purgation, illumination, and union.	The negotiated and creative transmission of culture through using its artifacts (language, art, music, etc.).
Whose work it builds on	MacIntyre	Christian mystical tradition, historians of spiritual exercises (e.g., Foucault, Hadot)	Bourdieu, de Certeau
Theological influences (and who is most comfortable with this formulation)	Roman Catholic neo-Thomism, Calvinism, Lutheranism, American Methodism	Roman Catholic monasticism, Anglicanism, classic Wesleyanism, Eastern Orthodoxy	Not specifically theological in focus.
Stresses	Communal formation in virtue	Deepening relationship with God	The interaction between the individual and society
Unique contributions	Conceptual richness. Links tradition, narrative, virtue, and practice.	Developmental and psychological sensitivity. Broad links to Christian tradition.	Helps describe the messiness and improvisation involved in everyday practice.
Limitations	Very specific notion of practice.	Can lose communal focus.	Can be so broad as to include every activity.

Commonalities in these approaches (Dorothy Bass):

1. Resist the separation of thought and action, doctrine and life.
2. See practices as social and historical.
3. See practices as rooted in the past but constantly adapting to changing circumstances.
4. See practices as articulating wisdom in the keeping of those who do not think of themselves as theologians.

Three Perspectives on Christian Practice[28]

Chapter Five

Seeing the Mainline Again

B etween 1994 and 2000, I wrote a weekly newspaper column on religion in America. Always on the hunt for good column material, I probably read every major news story written about American religion in those years. It was an amazing education in the diversity of contemporary religious practice. After awhile, however, I realized that the stories could be grouped into predictable categories. In a typical week, I read several stories about new religions in America (usually about the growth of Hinduism, Buddhism, or Islam) and equally as many on the influence of the Christian right in politics. Religious pluralism or Christian fundamentalism—religion journalists seemed interested in little else.

The Protestant mainline, my own tradition, seemed not to exist. The occasional mainline story tended to cover familiar territory: clergy sex scandals, division over homosexuality or women in leadership, and mainline decline. Journalists usually analyzed the event as if they were reporting congressional debate: "Conservatives within the Presbyterian church today blocked a resolution by liberals to change denominational policy regarding clergy marriage." Increasingly in the last two decades, every aspect of American culture—religious practice included—has been subsumed under a "left versus right" grid, the FOX News Channel view of the world.[1]

In many ways, this left–right media divide is odd because re-search suggests that many Americans—particularly adults born after 1960—feel increasingly uncomfortable with such polarization.[2] As a columnist and a churchgoer, left–right religion stories discomfort me. Despite the media hype around politically divisive issues, I have never actually attended a church where people split a congregation over the kinds of stories reported in the newspapers. Experience has taught me that even when churchgoers disagree about denominational or political concerns, they tend to stick with their local congregations. Disgruntled individuals might leave over women clergy or a gay elder. But rarely do national politics divide an entire church. On the local level, congregants function relationally—not like foot soldiers in a culture war.

Like all Americans, mainline Protestants may be politically conservative or politically liberal. On any given Sunday, the mainline Christians in America's pews hold a dizzying array of opinions on controversial theological and social issues. And, to a greater or lesser degree, they have learned (or are learning) to navigate their differences. The Zacchaeus Project, a study of the Episcopal Church, found that while there "are indeed serious differences," there are also "many instances of success at local levels in addressing them."[3] As researchers William Sachs and Thomas Holland write, "The single most surprising and remarkable impression upon our researchers . . . is that, in the final analysis, the form that conflict most often takes in the Episcopal Church seems more energizing than anxious, more collegial than adversarial, more hopeful than despairing."[4]

Like the thousands of interviewees in the Zacchaeus study, I have not been part of a congregation that fractured irrevocably over denominational politics. But I have, however, been a member of a church that divided over new worship music, moving the pews, changing the liturgy, and children in church! While denominational structures and national governing bodies may be more easily roiled by political intrigue, congregants on the local level tend to ignore such issues in favor of arguing over worship, architecture, prayer, children's education, and coffee hour.

Perhaps reporters find such conflicts dull, the wrangling of small-minded people with little else to do. Perhaps they do not consider such stories newsworthy. Perhaps they do notice these stories, but they have no way to interpret them. After all, moving candles from the altar obviously is not a "liberal versus conservative" thing—it has no culture-wars cachet. How then should we understand these "everyday" issues?

To outsiders, arguments over worship and Sunday school may seem trivial. However, they are not. These arguments are conflicts regarding religious practice, and, when properly understood and interpreted, they reveal a much deeper fissure in American spirituality than does the "liberal versus conservative" framework. Such conflicts expose a *practice continuum*—an often invisible field of expectations, style, and activities. The practice continuum exists in many mainline congregations as these churches struggle between the poles of *established* and *intentional* churchgoing. While church-goers may be more skilled at navigating liberal and conservative poles (or, perhaps, care less about them), the tensions between established and intentional styles are pronounced at the local levels. Yet many congregations are as blind to this continuum as their local religion reporter, as they fail to understand that the greatest tensions, challenges, and creativity in mainline churches are revealed in these conflicts.

The FOX News Mainline: Left versus Right

Although often overstated, a tension *does* exist between liberal and conservative forms of American Protestantism. In the late nineteenth and early twentieth centuries, Protestant churches endured a series of conflicts over theology known under the rubric of the fundamentalist-modernist controversy. Since that time, historians have posited a "two-party system" in American religion, where conservatives (a.k.a. evangelicals or fundamentalists) struggle with liberals (a.k.a. modernists or progressives) for political and theological control of Protestant denominations.[5]

In 1988, Princeton sociologist Robert Wuthnow suggested that the dominant conflict within American denominations is a contest between religious liberals and conservatives. "Liberals," he argued, "look across the theological fence at their conservative cousins and see rigid, narrow-minded, moralistic fanatics; conservatives holler back with taunts that liberals are immoral, loose, biblically illiterate, and unsaved."[6] Although Wuthnow recognizes the subtlety and texture of American religious life, he equally asserts that the "public image that came to characterize American religion in the 1980s was one in which deep polarization between two monolithic camps" dominated the media.[7]

Although "two monolithic camps" may be too strong a descriptor, most mainline churches do comprise two theological poles, typically called "liberal" and "conservative," and a host of blended possibilities along a continuum between the two.

The Left Pole

Today's mainline "left," variously called theological liberalism or progressivism, is the offspring of late-nineteenth-century Protestant liberalism. More than anything else, the liberal impulse was shaped by an acceptance of, and a desire to accommodate theologically to, modern culture and new sources of human experience and knowledge. According to historian Gary Dorrien, "The essential idea of liberal theology is that all claims to truth, in theology as in other disciplines, must be made on the basis of reason and experience, not external authority."[8] As a result, Protestant liberals could embrace scientific explanations for creation (especially those suggested by Charles Darwin), accept the findings of modern biblical scholarship, explore new philosophical interpretations of traditional Christian creeds, envision the human soul by incorporating insights from psychology, blend ideals of biblical justice with modern political systems and the new social sciences, and (eventually) rework engendered ministry roles as demanded by women's suffrage and feminism.

Throughout most of the twentieth century, Protestant liberalism was a powerful cultural force, even to the point of creating "a new theological establishment" in American churches and semi-naries.[9] Although liberalism changed over time, and not all liber-als believe the same things, those who identify with the Protestant left (or are the progeny of old-style liberalism) continue to share a sense of openness to contemporary culture, an emphasis on indi-vidual autonomy and religious experience, an understanding of Christianity as an "ethical way of life," and Jesus as (primarily) moral example, teacher, friend, or lover—traits of a theological worldview initially developed a century ago.[10] The Protestant left, despite its travails, modifications, and bad press, remains a prominent—if not dominant—way of being Christian in most mainline denomi-nations.

The Right Pole

The Christian right, then called by the self-designated term "fun-damentalism," developed as a reaction against liberalism in the late nineteenth and early twentieth centuries. Fundamentalism was shaped by a central belief in eternal and unchanging truth, "Jesus Christ, the same yesterday, today, and forever." To them, the Bible was God's literal word, without error in all things, a changeless theological handbook and moral guide. Thus, contemporary Prot-estant conservatives tend toward biblical literalism, believing that the Bible, a supernatural book, is clear and unambiguous in its teachings. These beliefs originally pushed conservative Protestants to "militant" anti-modernism, a "federation of co-belligerents united by their fierce opposition to modernist attempts to bring Christianity in line with modern thought."[11] Although some Ameri-can fundamentalists would eventually mute this combative ten-dency and opt to be called by the more genial moniker, "evangelicals," this oppositional stance remains strong in conser-vative Protestantism.

   In addition to sharing a literal approach to scripture, funda-mentalists and evangelicals emphasize salvation by faith in Jesus Christ alone through a personal experience of being "born again." This belief has created some tension between evangelical Protes-tants and traditional mainliners. More liberal mainline Protestants have tended to equate the rituals of baptism, confirmation, or living a moral life with salvation, believing that salvation is an act of the church in community instead of an individual decision to "follow Christ." In the Episcopal Church, for example, the greatest church crisis over fundamentalism occurred in the 1870s over baptism—not over biblical interpretation or creedal orthodoxy—when a group of conservatives protested the church's baptismal liturgy and left the mainstream Episcopal Church.[12]

Finally, conservative Protestants believe that salvation necessarily results in a piety of personal purity. As the old fundamentalist quip says, "I don't drink, dance, smoke, or chew and I don't go with boys who do." Although many have, in recent years, loosened up their attitudes toward specific things like dancing and drinking, conservative Protestants still mark the boundaries of their faith with particular behavioral choices believed to be revealed by scripture—being celibate until marriage, opposing abortion, voting Republican, and dressing modestly. Like liberals, not all conservatives believe the same things or act in the same ways. Even today, however, the "right" side of American Protestantism emphasizes the eternal truth of God's Word, exclusive salvation in Jesus Christ, and moral and sexual purity of the faithful believer.

A Theological Continuum

Since the late nineteenth century, when the two parties were birthed in tension and conflict with one another, national-level church politics has often been a struggle between the two impulses that Wuthnow described. The media, and often the partisans themselves, tend to see these impulses as two camps or warring parties, separate and isolated from one another, with little gray area in the middle:

Liberals **|** Conservatives

Long after the original fundamentalist-modernist controversy, denominations continue to fight along these lines today. Even as I was writing this chapter, my own denomination, the Episcopal

Church, was playing out an argument over the election and consecration of that church's first openly gay bishop. On the evening news, denominational conservatives and liberals debated the issue—portraying one another in less-than-flattering terms. The conservatives appealed to the literal sense of the scripture and moral purity; the liberals interpreted scripture through the lenses of culture, history, experience, and reason. Each remained true to its historical form. And to outsiders, it surely appeared that the church must be at war with itself.

On the August Sunday when the denomination's governing board was scheduled to vote on the issue, my family went to church. During the service, the congregation prayed for the church's national meeting and its leaders. No one got into an argument; no one left the church in a huff. The touch of politics was light and we got down to the real business of being church—listening to a sermon on "manna in the wilderness," singing hymns, and welcoming the strangers in our midst. That morning, congregants were gay and straight, young and old, black and white, rich and poor. We were there to be fed by God and to witness to the power of God's love in forming community in a fractured world.

Like the people at my church, most churchgoers do not understand themselves as partisans in some internecine war. In the pews, people do not typically identify with camps or parties, but tend to hold blended views on a variety of issues. Outside the world of national politics, American Protestants tend to get along on a local level even around the most divisive of issues.[13] Even at the height of the fundamentalist-modernist controversy, this was true as well—a whole host of centrist and moderate positions developed that challenged the far poles.[14] Where some observers see party warfare, better-informed interpreters see a line, with a variety of blended and moderated stances in between:

Liberals $\longleftrightarrow$ Conservatives

Despite the hype they receive on television, the pure form of these polarities rarely exists outside of the rarified worlds of advocacy and pundits. Studies of cultural conflict suggest that, depending upon the issues, approximately 10 percent of people reside at each pole. That means 80 percent of us hold views somewhere along the line—positions that blend, borrow, and accommodate from the poles! Simply reading contemporary spiritual autobiographies proves the point: In this popular genre, much of the narrative power comes from the struggles of individuals who are unwilling to identify with any "camp," and instead find God in places outside—or beyond—the poles.[15]

Although, as some scholars believe, "left" and "right" do describe a particular level of denominational conflict, these are increasingly unhelpful terms to understand American religious life, as new, blended stances emerge in Protestantism.[16] As Columbia University professor Randall Balmer so bluntly put it, "It is time to declare that the two-party paradigm is dead, or at least dysfunctional; if nothing else, the postmodern context cries out for a new paradigm."[17]

Out of the Historical Deep Freeze

At a point of crisis in my own life, a small church in Chapel Hill, North Carolina taught me a big lesson. Having attended an evangelical college and seminary, I had become a partisan, a person who spiritually and intellectually resided at the conservative pole. While in graduate school, questions began to "pull" me away from that camp and I began to move around on the line. All of this, combined with some personal issues, resulted in a spiritual and intellectual crisis—something not easily resolved.

The little church was called Church of the Holy Family. There, I experienced the serious practice of Christian faith through such simple things as hospitality, spiritual housekeeping, Bible study, and singing. These practices began to heal my soul as I could envision Christian life as something beyond dogma, something beyond theological culture wars. Church was about being a community of practice, a place where people learned the art of a way of life through discernment, prayer, and the Christian story as it unfolded through the grace of the church year. Holy Family comprised people on the theological left, people in the center, and people on the right. But it was rarely about one's *opinion* of faith. The community was about the loving *practice* of faith. As I would later write, "The simplicity of the parish, with its kind people and its practice of faith in daily life, put the pieces back together for me. . . . At Holy Family I began to sense the contours of a faithful life—one not defined by strict doctrines and moral certainty but one lived in true friendship and daily practice."[18]

Reflecting on Holy Family's corporate life did more than resolve my own personal spiritual crisis, however. It suggested to me that a different kind of mainline congregation than I had previously known was coming into existence. A Methodist church in Baltimore had shaped my childhood in the 1960s, particularly the ways in which that congregation organized and expressed their faith. With its emphasis on parish hall and home, and the ideal of the church as a civic organization, I first learned mainline church in the kind of "social congregation" that Brooks Holifield described in his congregational history periodization.[19]

Holy Family was a very different kind of congregation from my childhood Methodist church. Through my experiences there, I began to understand that something strange happened in mainline Protestantism in the twentieth century. As Protestant theology "froze" around the fundamentalist-modernist controversy, the Protestant vision of congregations also "froze" around the social congregation of the same period. The years 1870 to 1950 proved so successful for the Protestant mainline that both the theology and the congregation patterns *of that time* were enshrined as *the* tradition of "the Protestant establishment." Because of their very success, the traditions of established Protestantism lost the flexibility and creativity of earlier generations. Did such inflexibility lead to the decline of the 1960s? And, as a result, could the second half of the twentieth century, with that decline and its conflicts, be understood as a thawing-out of the old patterns—and the development of a new culture of being church?

Established Churchgoing

Perhaps because I was born in Baltimore, I resonate with Anne Tyler's books. Of her writing, a reviewer once remarked, "in Anne Tyler's fiction, family is destiny."[20] Tyler's book *The Accidental Tourist* tells the story of Macon, a man who glories in the familiar and insulates himself from anything foreign, who settles "in the grooves of neighborhood and habit," impervious to change.[21] Yet, oddly enough, Macon is a travel writer, an "accidental tourist," who writes guidebooks for people who hate to travel and want only to know the comforts of home while on the road.

From my Baltimore childhood, I understand family destiny, neighborhood, and habit. And I first experienced mainline Protestant churchgoing as the religious expression of seemingly change-less, inherited patterns—a kind of "accidental church." Before the mid-1960s, when everything (including Baltimore) began to change, American Protestantism was about family tradition, local community, and God's comfortable familiarity. Robert Wuthnow terms this ethos "dwelling spirituality," the religious impulse of being "at home with God."[22] Churchgoing was, like travel for Anne Tyler's Macon, an accident of sorts—something one did by virtue of being born in a particular family. Church was about the comfort of the familiar, not the challenge of the foreign.

Accidental churchgoing was the pattern of the mainline Protestant establishment—a style of religious practice that dominated religion for much of the twentieth century. Established Protestantism was marked by its chapel orientation: Church was a place to go where a minister performed certain spiritual tasks for the congregants (who usually inherited the faith from parents). Chapel religion typically blesses the social order, comforts people in times of crisis, and trains children in the customs of faith. It assumes that the surrounding culture is friendly and supportive of the congregation—which tends to be a homogeneous, closed system. Chapel-style churches are routinized organizations, where members *receive* customs, traditions, and beliefs rather than create new ones. They are places of family destiny, neighborhood, and habit.

Chapel-style churchgoing can be a compelling vision for tightly knit communities where congregations serve as an important part of local culture and provide places of refuge for certain social groups (typically in rural, immigrant, or poor communities). This model dominated much of American Protestant history and "worked" for a long time in relation to particular social structures. And it was the vision of church enshrined by those social congregations of the late nineteenth century.

This style was not theological: Protestants practiced this pattern regardless of denomination. Established churchgoing might be liberal or conservative because theology is not a determinative factor. The essence of established churchgoing was that one assumed denominational loyalty, received certain beliefs and practices from earlier generations with few questions, and expected these patterns to continue indefinitely. Indeed, to break the pattern revealed a certain kind of familial disloyalty, and religious conversion was socially fatal. And, like the characters in an Anne Tyler novel, family loyalty is one of the highest values in this worldview.

Intentional Churchgoing

If Anne Tyler's *Accidental Tourist* describes the world of established churchgoing, a religious universe of accidental habit, Anne Lamott's spiritual autobiography, *Traveling Mercies,* unpacks the vision of intentional churchgoing. Unlike the fictional Macon, nothing in Lamott's world, that of the San Francisco baby boomer spiritual seeker, is taken for granted. "My coming to faith did not start with a leap," she writes, "but rather a series of staggers from what seemed like one safe place to another . . . Each step brought me closer to the verdant pad of faith on which I somehow stay afloat today."[23]

According to Lamott, faith is not accidental. It is a purposeful relationship. Quoting Jewish theologian Martin Buber, she suggests that "all actual life is encounter," encounters with others, with our truest selves, and with God—encounters to which we must pay attention and engage purposefully. She depicts faith as an intentional pilgrimage, travel to a "foreign" place where one is changed by the encounter. For Lamott, the journey takes her home to a surprisingly traditional place—a small Presbyterian church (the denomination to which her grandparents belonged). But she got there through a route unrecognizable to previous generations of Presbyterians—a route described by poet T. S. Eliot as an exploration that leads back to "where we started and know the place for the first time."[24]

There is little new, of course, about American seeker religion. Historians have long noted that in the New World personal choice replaced inherited traditions. From the time of settlement, when European religion was, as historian Nathan Hatch noted, "democratized," to the rampant individualism of what sociologist Robert Bellah dubbed "Sheila-ism," Americans have chosen, shaped, and sometimes even invented their own personal religions and spiritual practices.[25] However, intentional churchgoing differs from individualized American religion in that it is a *corporate* journey. In recent years, it appears that the pilgrimage impulse, usually manifested in individual lives, has begun to characterize some churches— thus creating a pattern of intentional churchgoing.[26]

Intentional congregations are marked by mobility, choice, risk, reflexivity, and reflection. They think about what they do and why they do it in relation to their own history, their cultural context, the larger Christian story found in scripture and liturgy, and in line with the longer traditions of Christian faith. In addition to *thinking about* their practices, they reflexively engage practices that best foster their sense of identity and mission. Wade Clark Roof identified a pattern of "reflexive spirituality" among *individual* baby boomers. Quoting a fellow sociologist, Roof says:

> Reflexive spirituality involves . . . a "contemplative act of stepping back from one's own perspective and recognizing that it, too, is situated" in a plurality of possibilities. This capacity of understanding one's own view as just that—*a view*—forces attention to biography, history, and experience. Such awareness . . . encourages a profound sociological imagination . . . [whose] effect is to create greater self-engagement with religious tradition.[27]

Moving beyond Roof's analysis of individual reflexive spirituality (the kind described by Anne Lamott), it appears that *commu-*

nal reflexive spirituality is reshaping mainline Protestant congregations through the exercise of theological imagination (rather than "sociological" imagination) and corporate engagement with the practices of the longer Christian tradition. Roof suggests that this pattern of reflexive seeking might actually be "a creative, revitalizing experience" that could transform religious traditions—including religious congregations themselves.[28]

The accidental practices of established churchgoing assume insider status (the parishioner, or his or her family, has been part of the community for a long time) and often display low-demand characteristics in terms of spiritual rigor. The minister, a paid professional, typically performs religious tasks on behalf of the community. In contrast, intentional practices assume nothing about status—and they cost something in terms of choice, commitment, and involvement. In intentional congregations, this costliness creates a palpable sense of communal discipleship, mentoring, mutual learning, and spiritual formation; a pilgrim sensibility of people traveling together in community, whose practices embody a particular way of life in the world. In contrast to the chapel orientation of established churchgoing, the primary model for intentional congregations is faith-as-pilgrimage, a dynamic and organic image of mobility and change while fixing on an ultimate destination—union with God.

A Practice Continuum

When I served as the director of adult education, my conflict with Susan Noble helped to define notions of tradition—and rival traditions—within a congregation. The argument also highlights a conflict along the continuum between establishment-type understandings of the congregation and intentional ones. I am an intentional churchgoer, a person who experiences "church" as a reflexive way of being. Susan Noble was an established churchgoer who defined church primarily in terms of membership, a kind of religious civic organization. I wanted to offer a course on "the practice of peace," a series that I hoped would meet the congregation's spiritual needs; she wanted to continue a congregational event that

raised money to give to the poor. We each had different expectations about the nature and characteristics of Christian community—based in differing visions of church. Given these differences,
the conflict was inevitable.

Although the two styles are distinct in image, role of the
congregant, orientation, and goals, like the liberal–conservative
tension, they rarely exist as pure forms. Instead, many congregations can locate themselves somewhere along this continuum. Because of larger cultural pressures, I suspect that most are in a
process of moving from established churchgoing to the emerging
style of intentional church.

As the congregation itself shifts its identity, some parishioners
will go along while others may maintain the established patterns.
So, this continuum, like the other, may have multiple layers—a
layer of corporate identity and vision, a layer of identity and vision of individual congregants, and a layer of clergy identity and
vision. While the whole institution may be changing, the experience of that change may differ depending upon one's individual
place along the continuum.

Established

Intentional

My argument with Susan Noble was more than a disagree-
ment between two individuals with theologically divergent ideas
of church. It was also a congregational conflict over established
versus intentional churchgoing—she was trying to maintain the
established style of congregational life while I, along with some of
the clergy, attempted to push the congregation in a more intentional direction. In the last two decades, many congregations have
found themselves embroiled in conflict along these poles as the

t the same time, those who grew up within conservative Prot-
ism began a similar process of self-critique and internal theo-
l engagement, having become frustrated with an "evangelical
e" that was "insular, self-congratulatory, and often, embar-
" and that was "smothering Jesus in a heap of trivialities."[32]
angelicalism has shifted the locus of authority away from
ds of propositional truth so valued by conservatives to rela-
nd experiential forms of authority—thus opening the door
ts, questions, and ambiguity as legitimate parts of the spiri-
. (Interestingly enough, as I was preparing this manuscript,
cLaren, one the leading proponents of post-evangelicalism in
ed States, was finishing a book entitled *Generous Orthodoxy*,
g the same kind of open-yet-committed stance found in
alism, but directed toward a different audience).

as postliberalism is not a conversion to evangelicalism,
gelicalism should not be viewed as a conversion to liberal-
er, it is an internal development from one side of the Prot-
ide. In the cases of postliberalism and post-evangelicalism,
of each are critiquing their own cultures in light of both
communities' historical experience and the larger cul-
ures of detraditionalization. In the process, they have
a kind of ironic convergence—one that makes both tra-
erals and traditional evangelicals nervous and suspicious.
ew people anticipated amid the theological develop-
ever, was that postliberalism and postevangelicalism
me more than theological revolts in the ranks. It ap-
hey have also developed into congregational styles—
s where Christian tradition is intentionally practiced
e. From the postliberal side, George Lindbeck, Stanley
illiam Willimon, Loren Mead, Craig Dykstra, and An-
on have offered early—and suggestive—glimpses of
eral congregations might be like. Among post-
ome congregations have begun experimenting with
al styles—and pastors like Brian McLaren, Dan
Pagitt, Chris Seay, and Tony Jones have written about
gregations are changing. Eventually, perhaps inevi-

Ideals and Characteristics	Established Congregations	Intentional Congregations
Image	Chapel	Community
God	Father, Ruler, Judge, "Above Us"	Love, Spirit, "With Us"
Congregants	Members, family	Companions, pilgrims, friends
Ministry	Paid professionals	Shared, mentoring, teaching
Education	Information about Christian faith	Formation in Christian practices
Theology	Seminary-based, expertise	Communal task, lived, experiential
Piety	Introverted, private, devotional	Extroverted, expressive, spirituality
Orientation	Received, routinized, rules	Reflexive, reflective, risk
Space	Dwelling, structures, place	Fluid, dynamic, journey
Tradition	Deposit, inheritance, custom	Process, wisdom, flexible
Worldview	Compartmentalized, low tension with culture	Connected, medium-to-high tension with culture
Goal	Preservation, maintenance, salvation	Encounter, movement, way of life

Contemporary Congregations: The Established/Intentional Continuum

nature and expectations of church have changed in relation to larger cultural tensions. Conflicts along the practice continuum usually appear as arguments over worship, architecture, mission, vision, pastoral care, leadership, structure, ministry roles, and Christian education—not typically in arguments over the Bible, creeds, or ethics.

Instead of the old liberal–conservative divide, Protestantism is better understood as having four points of reference: two along the theological continuum of liberal and conservative; and two along the practice pole of established and intentional. These points create a grid of four congregational types where individual churches might be placed.

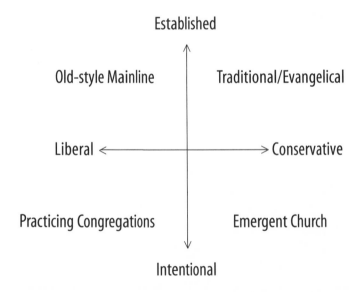

A Three-Dimensional Grid?

Not long ago, I was explaining this grid to a clergy group who labored in a judicatory fractured by their bishop's commitment to a culture-wars view of the church. Many of those attending the workshop were under forty-five. They were excited by the practice continuum because it reflected their own experiences in ministry. And seeing the church in a new way offered the possibility of moving

beyond the official drone of conflict iss⌄ office. During the lively discussion time, o⌐ "You know, the greater the level of inten⌐ blurring of the line between liberal and ⟨ of fact, I think intentionality trumps th⌐ The more committed we are to Chris⌐ we have in common. As your grid mo⟨ pole, I wish you'd get rid of the liber⌐ altogether!"

Although I think the liberal–con⌐ historically valid, I largely agreed with⌐ tions that have moved toward an in⌐ tice continuum—whether "liberal" o⌐ in common. And there is a good re⟨

The liberal–conservative divide⌐ philosophy.[29] In the last two or th⌐ theologians have questioned, chall⟨ rejected the theological assumpti⌐ conservative arguments. From e⟨ theologians have toiled to work⌐ Thinkers who had grown up w⌐ their theological perspectives ⌐ postmodern world. They have⌐ riety of "postliberal" theologic⌐ tion to the internal structu⌐ expressing unabashed "deligh⌐ tradition."[30]

Although postliberalism⌐ a kind of intellectual conve⌐ independent, constructive⌐ cal liberalism "to revisit C⌐ what might be wrong with⌐ redefine or illuminate cu⌐ terized postliberalism as⌐ combines the openness ⟨⌐ tian particularity.

tably, people from either side of the divide would meet—usually by reading one another's books or through actual engagement with particular practices.

Thus, postliberalism and postevangelicalism represent theological developments that move *off* or *beyond* the line and that move *toward* one another by virtue of their common self-critical stance and their reengagement with larger patterns of historic Christian tradition and practice. Thus, these movements help create a *multidimensional grid* for "reading" American Protestantism:

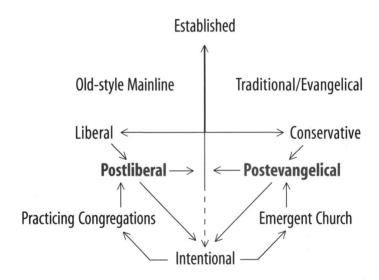

Imagine that you are no longer looking at a flat page in a book. Rather, the postliberal and postevangelical positions have jumped off the page toward you and create a layer of multidimensionality beyond the liberal–conservative line. With this grid, it becomes more apparent not only that the "posts" are protests against old-style theological liberalism and evangelicalism, but, in their shift toward intentionality, that these groups have also rejected traditional mainline (and evangelical) ways of defining and being the church. Seen this way, they create a new conversation circle—a place not bounded by theological lines, but a place of institutional boundary crossing. And although I am not entirely convinced the liberal–conservative line disappears, the minister at the workshop identified something that is often the case: Intentionality about practice has the potential to *lift* a congregation out of the old theological divide.[33] And it represents a cultural revolt against older styles of congregational organization.

Understanding Protestant congregations is not about left versus right; it is a challenging task of siting congregations in a multilayered grid with sets of tensions and possibilities based in both Protestant history and contemporary change.

Reframing the Stories

For three years, I lived in the Episcopal diocese of West Tennessee, a small judicatory with slightly more than thirty congregations and a big conservative reputation. Indeed, the majority of the congregations were conservative (a number still held deep reservations about women clergy) theologically and on social issues. Only a minority—four congregations—in the diocese defined themselves as theologically liberal (or moderate leaning toward liberal). There was, however, something odd about those four. They were the largest, richest, and fastest-growing churches in the diocese. Other more conservative churches were struggling and declining, often financially supported by the wealthier, more liberal ones.

In 1972, sociologist Dean Kelley wrote a book about mainline membership loss entitled *Why Conservative Churches Are Growing*. He argued that mainstream churches made no demands on members and declined, and, conversely, sectarian churches made demands and grew. The more demanding a faith, the greater its growth. Kelley's thesis was straightforward, and, in the opinion of many scholars, correct: Religiously demanding—that is, "strict"— churches grow.

However, Kelley's book was popularly interpreted to mean that *only* theologically conservative churches could be spiritually rigorous. Therefore, conservative theology was the determining factor in church growth. The more evangelical the message, the more people would join. Mainline liberal churches, therefore, were in a kind of theological and spiritual dead end. Kelley equated "conservative" with "demanding," or religion that had to be engaged with rigor and purpose.

Since Kelley's book first appeared, and even though it has been modified and refuted, the popularized versions of his thesis have dominated the way in which American Protestantism is analyzed in religious studies programs, seminary classrooms, denominational headquarters, "renewal" and advocacy organizations, and newsrooms. It reinforced the experience of two generations of American churchgoers—that the "big story" of American religion remained a kind of theological culture war, that conservatives, perhaps ironically, are predestined to win. Thus, every religious conflict is seen, as it has been seen since the late nineteenth century, as part of a war for the soul of American Protestantism.

But the Kelley thesis fails to explain the Episcopal diocese of West Tennessee. And it equally fails to explain the isolated growth and vitality of individual mainline congregations across the country. What Kelley did not see—and perhaps could not see—was the development of spiritual intentionality on the liberal side of the axis, the quadrant I call "intentional practice." There, people shaped by liberal Protestantism have reengaged Christian tradition and practice in ways that provide meaning, make demands on congregants, and strengthen commitment to living as God's people in the world. No one expected that old mainline churches would—or could—ever reject the low-demand, establishment ethos of the early twentieth century.

In each of the more liberal-leaning congregations in West Tennessee, parishioners were expected to engage practices of hospitality, prayer, social justice, spiritual formation, healing, inclusion, and studying the Word. While still being politely mainline about it, they nevertheless "demanded" certain things from their members—not in terms of doctrinal assent, but in terms of stewardship, spiritual growth, ministry, mission, and practice. According to Kelley,

such congregations could not exist. But they did. They were growing. And their growth far outpaced that of the more conservative
congregations.

In their book *Re-forming the Center*, Douglas Jacobsen and William Trollinger state: "No one can dispute that American Protestantism is terribly diverse and, often, just plain baffling. Yes, there
are patterns in American Protestant life and history, but these
patterns overlap and combine, conflict and diverge, and intensify
and fade in a host of complicated and unpredictable ways."[34] For
more than thirty years, mainline clergy, lay people, scholars, and
observers have forced American church life under the rubric of a
single pattern that reduces the creativity and complexity of religious experience—of the Holy Spirit in their midst—into a FOX
News paradigm.

What most ministers and church people know, however, is
that the liberal-versus-conservative continuum does not begin to
describe God's reality in the pews. In those same thirty years, the
experience of mainline church has been changing. That other line,
the practice continuum, has been the locus of intense re-formation,
renewal, and rebirth in unexpected and surprising ways.

Chapter Six

I Love to Tell the Story

In late 2003, many reporters called asking me to comment on the Episcopal Church's election of Gene Robinson, a man in a committed gay partnership, to be the bishop of New Hampshire. One particular journalist drilled me with a long list of predictable questions about denominational liberals and conservatives. Finally, she said, "Isn't this whole episode just one more reason the mainline is in decline?"

"Mainline decline?" I chuckled into the receiver.

"What's so funny?" she asked.

"Well, I'm working on a study right now of mainline Protestant vitality where I'm in conversation with fifty of the most interesting, energetic, creative, and lively congregations I've ever had the privilege of knowing. They don't fit in your categories. They are the cutting edge of mainline life. And, because of them, I forget that people believe in something called 'mainline decline.' I just don't see that anymore."

I went on to talk about rival traditions and an emerging style of practicing congregations. The flabbergasted reporter did not know what to say.

What happened to me? Why couldn't I conceptualize the problem she did? By pressing past conventional wisdom regarding congregations, I had been engaged in an imaginative rethinking of

American Protestantism. In the process of opening my own imagination, I had come to understand the longer patterns of history, the tensions around cultural change, the conflicts of traditions and fluid retraditioning, and had crafted the accepted interpretation into a more nuanced model. All of this was interlaced with my own experience of congregations and intuitions about ministry. The tools of the scholar combined with an act of theological imagination.

In his book *Ministry and Imagination*, the late theologian Urban T. Holmes argues that "man is not just a creature who thinks analytically and logically, but his very biology indicates that he has the capacity to exercise a creative imagination. We can speak of the effect of this imagination in terms of *seeing* the deeper meaning of our experience, as opposed to merely looking upon the surface."[1] Holmes concretizes this by telling the story of a friend leaving Los Angeles one night:

> As the plane lifted off the ground, it moved through this noxious layer of particulate, and suddenly, as it rose above the clouds, he and his fellow travelers became aware as if for the first time of a world of translucent beauty, filled with a quarter moon, stars, and distant lightning. Not until he moved above the smog did he realize how the by-products of our industrial system had closed in his whole perception of the world, and that his understanding of his experience was subject to such a degree to the system within which he lived."[2]

For the last three decades, many mainline Protestants have experienced congregational life subject to "the system" within which we live. Holmes continues, "It is important for us to realize that the social system . . . reduced the meaning of our experience to one- and two-dimensional categories."[3] Thus, the larger cultural stories about mainline churchgoing—decline, irrelevance, and ennui—appear to have inhibited vitality by flattening transcendent aspects of congregational life into categories that are "secular, disenchanted, and oriented to production and consumption."[4]

A couple of years ago, I interviewed members of Trinity Episcopal Church, a mainline congregation that had experienced a surprising turn-around. Threatened by shrinking membership rolls, financial problems, and even the wrecking ball, the church had found new life in a revitalized sense of identity through Christian practices, social justice, and shared leadership. When I asked some congregants what had happened, they had trouble answering the question. One remarked, "It is all very mysterious. The power of the Spirit, I think." Another added, "We found the numinous awe [in one another]." Over the years, I have come to believe that the congregation was able to imagine a different way of being church and committed themselves to making it happen. They refused to be "flattened" by the story of mainline decline. Instead, as one lay leader commented to me, "We did it. We've created the kind of church we only dreamed existed back in the 1960s. And here it is."[5]

Trinity's story is so remarkable that I have often used it as an example in lectures or at professional conferences. While colleagues and clergy can appreciate that congregation's experience, they also express doubts that Trinity can serve as any kind of model to "normal" churches. "It is too fluky," one commented, "because it is in California." A different protest: "The people are too peculiar." A prominent sociologist of religion once said to me, "It is a nice story, but meaningless because it can't be replicated. No one else can use it."

Something odd happens, however, whenever I tell the story of Trinity in nonprofessional settings, like bookstore readings or adult education forums. *People cry.* For a brief moment, listeners experience someone else's story—a story that enables them to see past the surface, a story that lifts them above the thick level of cultural haze and helps them imagine a better, different way of being church. Standing up at Barnes & Noble and reading to total strangers about finding the "numinous awe" in a quirky Episcopal congregation has taught me something important: People want to soar above the smog. They want to see. They want to find an enchanted world.

This is more than romantic wistfulness. The act of imaging new, exciting possibilities is fundamental to being human. "Our brains are built to create and play with images," claims professor David Hogue, "brains by their very structures have the capacity to create and reshape images they take in."[6] Hogue goes on to argue that understanding the brain's natural imaginative processes are key to pastoral theology and spiritual vitality. "Imagination frees us from the tyranny of the present, of the logical, of the 'real,'" he explains. "It also frees us from the constraints of the now, as it pictures what events were like in the historic past or what they might become in the future."[7] He further suggests both that Christian practices are supported by the imagination and that the Christian imagination is strengthened through communal participation in practices.[8] As I argued earlier, understanding faith as a "chain of memory" that imaginatively links past, present, and future through renewed attention to practice dovetails with Hogue's work on theology, imagination, and the brain. We have the capacity to live *beyond* the "mere facts" of mainline decline—and the spiritual obligation to free ourselves from the tyranny of the FOX news story of the present. People—even those in the anonymous Barnes and Noble audience—intuit the relationship between imagination, spirit, and Christian community and long for fresh images of hope.

Urban Holmes suggested that imagination is an act of pilgrimage—of going "outside the city" to find God's presence.[9] "The city" may be the accepted way of doing things, listening to the approved narrative, following the proven program. Yet, the development of the emerging congregational style outlined in this book points to the imaginative power of congregations to move beyond normative patterns and programmatic fixes into a place of doing and being church that embodies the enchantment of the Christian story in the practices of faith. And that is what this book has been all about: to assert that the *pastoral imagination* and the *congregational imagination* can reflexively harmonize to become more truly church—the human witness to God's kingdom, the reality that gives ultimate meaning to earthly existence.

And it is not a fantasy to say so. As Holmes argues, "Imagination *builds* on facts, truth, and reality. Unlike fantasy . . . it moves forward by a judicious selection and reshaping of the representations of experience that make up our meaning."[10] In every generation of Christian history, faithful congregations have selected and reshaped tradition, developing patterns that reflect transcendent realities in ways that speak to the surrounding culture. That some contemporary mainline congregations in the United States are finding their path to such new patterns should be no surprise. From the perspective of history, it would be far more surprising if they *failed* to rework their traditions and practices. Failing to do so would surely result in "decline."[11]

Mainline Protestant congregations of the 1950s were not bad places—they were vibrant, successful, growing congregations that met the needs of people at a particular moment in American history. Imagination created social congregations and participatory congregations in the first place. Because of their very success, however, they lost the capacity to imagine church being different than how they experienced it and, essentially, froze tradition in its tracks. The lack of imaginative and fluid retraditioning in a new cultural world "caused" mainline decline. After all, imaginatively fiddling around with tradition is one of things that congregations do.

Storytelling, Imagination, Tradition, and Practice

In *Ministry and Imagination*, Holmes provides a helpful example of fiddling around with tradition:

> In the conclusion of *Fiddler on the Roof* the question is asked from off stage, "What holds him [the fiddler on the roof] up?" The answer is heard, "Tradition." This is what I mean. The creativity of "fiddling around" is possible when it is done within the ongoing self-consciousness of a community, which we call tradition. It is the sense of identity, handed down through time (the Greek word for tradition, *paradosis*, means to "hand down"), which gives us the imagery and the security to think the new.[12]

Tradition is embodied in practices. And practices convey meaning through narrative. Without stories, tradition and practice would mean either nothing or anything. And stories—both about the past and the future—are crafted through the imagination. What Holmes calls "the ongoing self-consciousness of a community," what I have called congregational intentionality, is carried through and by story, fueled by imaginative vision, embodied in practice and passed through time by tradition.

For the same thirty years that the old Protestant mainline has been suffering under the weight of decline, theologians have been developing new understandings of theology and story under the general rubric of narrative theology. Narrative theology assumes that scripture tells a story, that faith communities live into and interpret that story, and that individual believers make sense and meaning in relation to those stories.[13] In *After Virtue*, Alistair MacIntyre, who has deeply influenced thinking about Christian practices, links tradition, practice, and narrative into "a mutually supporting and interlocking web of concepts" in which human beings locate themselves in a larger purpose, or *telos* (meaning "consummation").[14]

Much of the effort in narrative theology has been toward understanding the Christian story itself; some has been toward how believers live in relation to the story; and some has been a reflexive exploration of the relationship between story and believer. "We receive our true story," claims theologian John Navone, "our authentic identity, from the God—the Storyteller—who wills or intends it for us. Our reception or finding of our true story— what we ultimately become in accordance with the grace and demand of God—is by no means a purely passive event; rather, it demands our full collaboration and effort."[15] For narrative to achieve its fullest strength as an approach to theology and life, it insists upon intentional, creative, reflexive engagement of tradition and practice.

Beyond the construction of individual faith lives, however, such theological engagement has often appeared to float disconnected from larger structures of meaning-making. Despite talk about "the community of faith" or "Christian communities," narrative approaches tend to skip over *congregations* as the primary way in which Christians organize community. Many theologians seem to envision Christian community in some pure—almost disembodied— way that bears little relation to how most people experience faith through stories. Most Christians first hear the stories in congregations; they enact the stories in congregations; they tell the stories to their children in congregations.

One of the few exceptions to this was James Hopewell's influential book *Congregation: Stories and Structures*, which argued that congregational culture is "a coherent system whose structural logic is *narrative*."[16] According to Hopewell, congregations define themselves in narrative, they communicate by narrative, and they interact with the larger world through narrative. Their story gives them a distinctive identity and mission, the keys to vision, health, and vitality.

Although Hopewell's work has typically been utilized as a way to *study* congregations, it also lays out a path of congregational vitality—the more intentional a congregation is about its story (and the more honest, authentic, and coherent as well), the more likely it is to be a place of vital traditioning and practice. Dorothy Bass also suggests this: While all congregations tell stories, these stories often "recede into the background like familiar wallpaper, taken for granted but unexamined." She goes on to relate a story of congregational conflict and rebirth through a "process of deliberate and explicit inquiry into the congregation's understanding of its relation to God and, in the light of God, to others."[17] They had to learn—in this case, the hard way—their unique story.

Story takes us beyond where we are, giving us the ability to see past the haze. Ernest Kurtz and Katherine Ketcham state that, "Listening to stories and telling them helped our ancestors to live humanly—to *be* human. But somewhere along the way our ability to tell (and to listen to) stories was lost."[18] The recovery of story is essentially a spiritual act whereby individuals and communities find a sense of meaning and purpose in life. Attention to story is the basis of one contemporary form of therapy called narrative counseling. According to Joseph Stewart-Sicking, a pastoral theologian trained in this method, "narrative counseling is grounded in the assumption that the basic quality of human life is that it has a narrative shape—all of us have a story to tell. Thus, wholeness and healing are achieved by learning to tell the story of one's life in a new way with new understandings of the characters, new subplots, and new ways of making sense of what has happened."[19] Story heals and opens a new way for the client.

What if storytelling functioned in such a way for congregations? What if we understood that narrative is, as Hopewell indicated, the "basic quality" of congregational life? And, as Dorothy Bass pointed out, does that struggling for a new story indeed illuminate a path of new vitality? Imagination is the stage on which narrative, tradition, and practice perform their dance. It is not a matter of logical development of philosophical theology exercised in a congregation; it is an act of the faithful imagination of pastor and congregation collectively—and intentionally—moving around the circle of narrative, tradition, and practice. Tradition may hold him up, but imagination got that fiddler up on the roof in the first place.

Landing the Plane

Fiddlers, however, cannot stay up on roofs forever. Nor can planes always soar above the smog. Sooner or later, no matter how beautiful the view or invigorating the new perspective, the plane has to land.

Urban Holmes depicts the ministerial imagination as a pilgrimage into the place of "anti-structure," where risk, intuition, ambiguity, uncertainty, and creativity mark the way. "The anti-structure is the place of freedom to imagine," he claimed. "It confronts us with what is at the same time most frightening and most potentially creative: the stuff of chaos."[20] In the anti-structure a kind of spiritual death occurs—the willingness to let go of familiar structures and ways of being. Only through this "death" can one reenter the structure. But the reentry lands the pilgrim at a different place: at the periphery, a point where anti-structure (imagination and risk) and structure (order and security) meet. In literary terms, pilgrims come home different. They arrive back where they started and, in the words of T. S. Eliot, "know the place for the first time." Or, as G. K. Chesterton once quipped about his own conversion to Christianity, "I discovered England."[21]

If my assertion is correct that a new kind of mainline congregation has come into being, it means that this process of imagination and reintegration has already been underway in some congregations and with some clergy. Many of the congregations in my study have actually reported "near-death" experiences—crises of membership, money, vision, or leadership—that fostered imaginative processes already moving in the congregation. The ability to give up or surrender their received notions of church-as-institution provided a kind of spiritual entry point into creating new patterns of being church. In the case of these congregations, that meant reaching back into Christian history and appropriating and reworking traditions and practices that met contemporary challenges. To borrow Eliot again, their imaginative exploration led them home—and they knew that place for the first time.

Key to all this is good storytelling. Pilgrims, either an individual or group, who have journeyed into the place of imagination and risk, must be able to come home and relate the tale. They must be able to relate what they have seen—the view from the roof or the airplane window. They must be able to help others see what they have seen—opening the visionary possibilities of the whole community—and authentically embody the story that they have shared. They must show how the story transformed them.

"Leaders achieve their effectiveness chiefly through the stories they relate," asserts Harvard professor Howard Gardner. "In addition to communicating stories, leaders *embody* those stories."[22] A leader, he insists, is "a storyteller." David Fleming, director of the Emerging Leaders Institute, says that "through storytelling, the leaders can help the organization understand where it is within the ambiguity-opportunity cycle and what qualities it will need to undertake the current trek."[23] In relating stories, leaders call forth corporate imagination, creativity, and resources that enable the whole group to move forward and change.

Practicing congregations are storytelling congregations. Often, the formal stories told by means of preaching or teaching are told through the theological lens of narrative theology or the skills of narrative preaching. Congregations also tell stories through the practice of testimony. Long treasured in black churches and by evangelicals, testimony is being recovered by mainline congregations. At Church of the Redeemer in New Haven, Connecticut, a UCC congregation founded during the Second Great Awakening, congregants regularly reenact the ancient New England art of publicly witnessing to the work of the Holy Spirit in their lives as part of the worship service. In the last five years, careful attention to telling faith stories sparked renewal in the congregation and fostered broad enthusiasm to serve as lay leaders. Eventually, the church replaced their older "business model" of church with practices of spiritual leadership shaped by personal testimonies. In the process, the congregation both grew numerically and deepened spiritually—as they created a culture of leadership based on storytelling.[24]

On an informal level, congregants can also relate stories—intentional stories—of the congregation's journey in faith. In practicing congregations stories are not like "familiar wallpaper." Rather, they are self-conscious and imaginative tales that the community shares—not unlike stories told around campfires by generations of pilgrims past. Gardner insists that the primary skill for leaders is the ability to clarify and reconceptualize stories, essentially to be one of the best storytellers around the campfire: "It is important for leaders to know their stories, to get them straight, to communicate them effectively, particularly to those who are partial to rival stories, and above all, to embody in their lives the stories that they tell."[25]

Shared narrative leadership both lifts the plane and lands it. It allows people to see beyond the surface *and* it calls forth a community's gifts to make it happen. And it is easy to paraphrase Gardner's vision of vital leadership to a vision for vital congregations as a whole: *It is important for congregations to know their stories, to get them straight, to communicate them effectively, particularly to those who are partial to rival stories, and, above all, to embody in their lives the stories that they tell.*

Trinity Episcopal provides an example of this. The *congregation*—not a single leader—imagined a different kind of congregation. And, in many ways, getting there was "mysterious." But in other ways it was not. They imagined being an open community, one to which anyone and everyone could come and find God; they had a new sense of identity and vocation. They called new clergy leadership that, they hoped, would help them get to a new place. That new sense of identity and leadership, in turn, gave them the energy to conceptualize and execute an ambitious capital campaign that would save the building from being torn down.

They did not simply sit around and imagine. It was neither passive nor completely supernatural. Rather, imagination gave them a new story—and that spurred them to do what professional fundraisers told them might be impossible. The tiny, once dying congregation raised more than $1,000,000. Imaginations fired, they exceeded their goals and, in the process, doubled the size of their congregation, ensuring not only its physical continuation but also its health and vitality for some time to come.

Trinity further illustrates the processes of imagination, story, and leadership of practicing congregations. After raising the money and increasing its membership, some congregations may have thought, "Whew. That's over. We did it." Trinity did not. Instead, their communal imagination said, "Whew. That's over. What's next?" They moved—to use Holmes's concept—from structure (declining congregation) to anti-structure (imagining a new congregational identity and the risk of the fundraising campaign) to renewed structure (building renovation and a commitment to particular Christian practices) back to anti-structure (the imaginative process of seeing beyond the surface). This style of congregation does not really stop; they do not think that they have arrived. For them, the meaning of Christian community is found in the imaginative journey and the renewal of tradition—the pilgrimage of creating church.

But it is not just spiritual busywork. Throughout, Trinity has learned to emphasize practices of discernment and Sabbath-keeping, thus balancing the hard work of intentional imagination and fluid retraditioning with the rest and time provided by the very practices that they have introduced. The plane lands to be refueled or, perhaps, to tinker with the mechanics. These pilgrims understand that, in the contemporary world, the gospel means that one never finally arrives. You just keep telling stories along the way.

Imagine, for a moment, a new story about mainline Protestantism. What if the story wasn't about decline, division, and spiritual dismay? What if the story was about imaginative congregations reaching back to their native stories, drawing out practices known to their ancestors, and finding new ways of being faithful in a fragmented, detraditionalized world? What difference would that story make in your own ministry, your congregation, in your diocese or synod or presbytery, in the national offices of the denomination? How would that story challenge rival stories about mainline faith? What other new stories are waiting to be told? In the last two or three decades, mainline Protestants have been trying to land the plane before it had a chance to take off. Luckily, some congregations have been flying solo. But it may be time for a new, communal flight of imagination and new tales to tell of the journey.

Thus, this book ends not with a standard academic conclusion or a summary of its thesis. Rather, this exercise in theological imagination ends with a parable from a Jesuit missionary to India that points to the pitfalls of not seeing with the eyes of imagination—living in the same, tired narrative of mainline religion—or the wonders of seeing the new vistas of life:

> And here is a parable of life for you to ponder on: A group of tourists sits in a bus that is passing through gorgeously beautiful country; lakes and mountains and green fields and rivers. But the shades of the bus are pulled down. They do not have the slightest idea of what lies beyond the windows of the bus. And all the time of their journey is spent in squabbling over who will have the seat of honor in the bus, who will be applauded, who will be well considered. And so they remain till the journey's end.[26]

What if the journey is just beginning?

Afterword

I used to know someone who was a spy. I wasn't supposed to know this, but it was pretty obvious. He had been formed—not just as a spy, but as a person—in the cold war era. The Russians were the bad guys and Americans were the good guys. Certain words were always yoked together in this dualism: *capitalism/democracy/good/us* and *communism/socialism/bad/them*. When the Iron Curtain fell and the old Soviet Union deconstructed, it created a crisis for this person. He needed a new enemy. He found it hard to function in a more complex, less polarized world. He was disoriented.

Millions of Christians in America face a similar challenge. We've been formed in a world of religious dualism of liberal and conservative—perhaps we could call it "the lukewarm war." But if Diana Butler Bass is right in these pages, the landscape is changing and we must reorient. What will we do? Will we beat dead horses? Will we create a new dualism? Just as Islamic fundamentalism has replaced communism for our government as the "Evil Empire," the liberal–conservative religious cold war could morph into some new conflict, giving us ever-new outlets for our aggression and ever-fresh ways to justify our existence.

But this book has invited us to imagine a different future.

I am especially struck by a sentence in the last chapter: "Luckily, some congregations have been flying solo." These congregations have somehow found another way to define themselves and set their course. They haven't flown in the military formation of conservatives-against-liberals or liberals-against-conservatives. They haven't let their flight plan be set by air-traffic controllers working off of old maps that misrepresent the new landscape. They represent anomalies, maybe genetic mutations in the framework of evolutionary biology—and their unconventional, innovative, imaginative flights now offer new possibilities for the rest of us.

A parallel phenomenon has been happening in conservative evangelical circles. Yes, many conservative Protestant congregations fly in formation, or remain parked on the tarmac in good company with other stable, safe, earthbound souls. But a few break free and take off in unexpected directions. They emerge from the status quo and offer new possibilities.

This situation on both sides of the liberal–conservative spectrum creates many exciting possibilities. These innovative congregations can model new ways of being Christians and congregations for their respective tribes. *And they can resource one another.*

The fact is, there have long been elements on both sides that defy stereotypes. Long before mainline Protestants ordained women, for example, many Pentecostal and Holiness denominations had been doing so. Now, as more and more congregations refuse to fly in the old formations of the "lukewarm war" era, we face the possibility of new connections, new convergences, new alliances, new relationships. As Diana Butler Bass says, ". . . it may be time for a new, communal flight of imagination and new tales to tell of the journey."

Perhaps a good first step would be for readers of this book to call up a counterpart from a church in their area—a church of a different denomination, and perhaps a church from "the other side" of old polarities. Perhaps over a cup of coffee or some other mutually acceptable beverage, readers could share their stories and elicit the stories of others—stories of intrepid, quirky, far-from-perfect congregations seeking to bounce out of old ruts, congregations seeking to fly the plane higher and farther rather than land it and keep it safely grounded in the hangar.

Meanwhile, as postliberal and postconservative Protestants begin weaving their narratives, they need to keep a place at the table for their Roman Catholic and Orthodox friends as well, because I know pilots of a kindred spirit are revving their engines in those airlines too.

What could happen if, across the spectrum of Christian faith, wings stretch wide to catch a new, strong wind? The possibilities are breathtaking.

How tragic and boring, in comparison, to sit squabbling on the earthbound bus and miss the beauty and adventure. Some will take that option—staying earthbound, focusing on retirement plans and seats of honor, afraid to rock boats and forgetting that our Lord was unafraid to dispense with boats altogether and walk on water. How's that for an invitation to imagine impossible possibilities?

Brian D. McLaren

Notes

Introduction

1. Margaret R. Miles, "Image," in Mark C. Taylor, ed., *Critical Terms for Religious Studies* (Chicago: University of Chicago Press, 1998), p. 160.

2. Craig Dykstra, "The Pastoral Imagination," in *Initiatives in Religion 9*, no. 1 (Spring 2001): p. 2.

3. Ibid., 15.

4. James F. Hopewell, *Congregation: Stories and Structures* (Philadelphia: Fortress Press, 1987), p. 141.

Chapter One

1. Kit and Frederica Konolige, *The Power of Their Glory: America's Ruling Class: The Episcopalians* (New York: Wyden Books, 1978).

2. Few books make the point as clearly as Amanda Porterfield's work, *The Transformation of American Religion: The Story of a Late Twentieth-Century Awakening* (New York: Oxford University Press, 2001).

3. Although dozens of studies have examined these losses, the first book, Dean Kelley's *Why Conservative Churches Are Growing: A Study in Sociology of Religion* (New York: Harper & Row, 1972), remains symbolically important. Many scholars have refuted, disputed, or refined his arguments, but Kelley's thesis—that only conservative churches grow—maintains a stubborn hold on the public imagination regarding mainline religion.

4. The best example of this interpretation of American religious history is Diana L. Eck, *A New Religious America: How A "Christian Country"*

Has Become the World's Most Religiously Diverse Nation (San Francisco: HarperSanFrancisco, 2001). These developments are also covered in Randall Balmer and Lauren F. Winner, *Protestantism in America,* Columbia Contemporary American Religion Series (New York: Columbia University Press, 2002).

5. For a helpful analysis of membership "decline," see C. Kirk Hadaway, "Is the Episcopal Church Growing (or Declining)?" at http:// www. ecusa.anglican.org/documents/2004GrowthReport(1).pdf.

6. Diana Butler Bass, *Strength for the Journey: A Pilgrimage of Faith in Community* (San Francisco: Jossey-Bass, 2002); Robert A. Chestnut, *Transforming the Mainline Church: Lessons in Change from Pittsburgh's Cathedral of Hope* (Louisville: Geneva Press, 2000); Milton J. Coalter et al., *Vital Signs: The Promise of Mainstream Protestantism* (Grand Rapids, Mich.: Wm. B. Eerdmans, 1996); *The Zacchaeus Project: Discerning Episcopal Identity at the Dawn of the New Millennium* (New York: The Episcopal Church Foundation, 1999); Diana Butler Bass, "Mainline Incline," *Religion and Ethics Newsweekly* (January 26, 2001), transcript at http://www.pbs.org/wnet/religionandethics/transcripts/422.html.

7. See, among others: Nancy Tatom Ammerman, *Congregation and Community* (New Brunswick, N.J.: Rutgers University Press, 1997); Jackson W. Carroll, *Mainline to the Future: Congregations for the 21st Century* (Louisville: Westminster John Knox, 2000); Jackson W. Carroll and Wade Clark Roof, eds., *Beyond Establishment: Protestant Identity in a Post-Protestant Age* (Louisville: Westminster John Knox, 1993); C. Kirk Hadaway, *Behold I Do a New Thing: Transforming Communities of Faith* (Cleveland: Pilgrim, 2001); C. Kirk Hadaway and David A. Roozen, *Rerouting the Protestant Mainstream: Sources of Growth and Opportunities for Change* (Nashville: Abingdon, 1995); Donald E. Miller, *Reinventing American Protestantism: Christianity in the New Millennium* (Berkeley: University of California Press, 1997); and Robert Wuthnow, *After Heaven: Spirituality in American Since the 1950s* (Berkeley: University of California Press, 1998).

8. Howard A. Snyder, *The Problem of Wineskins: Church Structure in a Technological Age* (Downers Grove, Ill.: InterVarsity, 1975), p. 21.

9. For interesting surveys of the variety of congregational forms, see Mary Anne Reese, "Refracting the Light: The Broad Spectrum of Young Adult Catholics" in *America* (September 22, 2003) and reprinted in *Crossroads: A Publication of the Catholic Campus Ministry Association* (April/May 2004); and *Mission-Shaped Church: Church Planting and Fresh Ex-*

pressions of Church in a Changing Context (London: Church House Publishing, 2004), pp. 43–83. Although Reese's article is about Roman Catholic congregations and *Mission-Shaped* is a study of the Church of England, the forms described in each are readily identifiable in relation to American Protestantism.

10. Kelley, *Why Conservative Churches Are Growing*. For a self-congratulatory assessment of evangelical renewal in the mainline, see Michael S. Hamilton and Jennifer McKinney, "Turning the Mainline Around," at http://www.christianitytoday.com/ct/2003/008/1.34.html

11. Miller, *Reinventing American Protestantism*; Kimon Howland Sargeant, *Seeker Churches: Promoting Traditional Religion in a Nontraditional Way* (New Brunswick, N.J.: Rutgers University Press, 2000).

12. Loren B. Mead, *New Hope for Congregations* (New York: Seabury, 1972).

13. In his *After Heaven*, Robert Wuthnow comes close to suggesting the existence of practicing congregations by exploring the emergence of "practice-oriented spirituality" among individuals. See his discussion on pp. 168–98. Also, C. Kirk Hadaway describes a similar type as "incarnational community" in *Behold I Do a New Thing*.

14. See Rick Warren, *The Purpose-Driven Church: Growth without Compromising Your Message and Mission* (Grand Rapids, Mich.: Zondervan, 1995) and http://www.purposedriven.com. Rick Warren's church, Saddleback Community Church, outside San Diego, and Willow Creek Community Church, in suburban Chicago, are excellent examples of new paradigm intentionality, but they are not examples of the type identified here. For an interesting approach on the possibility of combining vitality types, see Brian D. McLaren, *The Church on the Other Side: Doing Ministry in the Postmodern Matrix* (Grand Rapids, Mich.: Zondervan, 2000).

15. "Alternatives to Institutional Religion Find Favor," *Religion Watch* 19 (May 2004): p. 7.

16. This is the author's definition. This paragraph, along with much of the section on the intentional practice type, was greatly enhanced and refined in conversations with Dorothy C. Bass, Director of the Valparaiso Project on the Formation of People of Faith at Valparaiso University in Indiana, Christopher Coble, an American religious historian who serves as a religion division program officer at Lilly Endowment Inc. in Indianapolis, my research associate, Joseph Stewart-Sicking, and faculty

colleagues at Virginia Theological Seminary, Jeff Hensley and Timothy Sedgwick.

17. E. Brooks Holifield, "Toward a History of American Congregations," chap. 1 in James P. Wind and James W. Lewis, eds., *American Congregations, Volume 2: New Perspectives in the Study of Congregations* (Chicago: University of Chicago Press, 1994), pp. 23–53.

18. This chart is based upon ibid. and Diana Butler Bass, *Strength for the Journey,* 271–81.

19. Holifield, *American Congregations,* 2:33–46.

20. In their book *Bridging Divided Worlds: Generational Cultures in Congregations* (San Francisco: Jossey-Bass, 2002), Jackson W. Carroll and Wade Clark Roof argue that new paradigm churches (sometimes referred to as "post-traditional" churches) constitute a new period in Holifield's scheme. I would like to suggest that new paradigm churches are both the last expression of the participatory congregation era and the first expression of a new period of congregational style, that of the "intentional congregation." Thus, new paradigm churches are a sort of generational hinge, a transitional form of organization in American congregational history.

21. See "Alternatives to Institutional Religion," in *Religion Watch* (May 2004).

22. In some ways, intentional congregations may be one religious expression of—or a parallel development to—the emerging "creative class," whose worldview is charted by Richard Florida, *The Rise of the Creative Class . . . and How It's Transforming Work, Leisure, Community and Everyday Life* (New York: Basic Books, 2002); and Paul H. Ray and Sherry Ruth Anderson, *The Cultural Creatives: How 50 Million People Are Changing the World* (New York: Three Rivers, 2000).

23. *Mission-Shaped Church,* pp. 43–83. In this study, churches grouped under "base ecclesial communities," "cell church," "café church," and the category bearing the unwieldy name, "traditional forms of church inspiring new interest," share characteristics with the style of practicing congregations suggested in this book.

24. Reese, "Refracting the Light." Reese's categories "The Church Apologist" and "The Church Devotional" resemble the mainline practicing congregation.

25. For more on the "emergent church" movement, see http://www.emergentvillage.org; for patterns of reorganization among evangelicals, see Robert E. Webber, *The Younger Evangelicals: Facing the Challenges of the New World* (Grand Rapids, Mich.: Baker, 2002).

Chapter Two

1. Not much research has been done on the difference between early- and late-cohort baby boomers. Yet the later boomers, born between 1955 and 1962, make up a sort of hinge generation between the 1960s and GenX postmodernism. The exception to this research omission is Wade Clark Roof, *A Generation of Seekers: The Spiritual Journeys of the Baby Boom Generation* (San Francisco: HarperSanFrancisco, 1993). For GenX spirituality, see Richard W. Flory and Donald E. Miller, eds., *GenX Religion* (New York and London: Routledge, 2000); and Tom Beaudoin, *Virtual Faith: The Irreverent Spiritual Quest of Generation X* (San Francisco: Jossey-Bass, 1998).

2. On the decline of the oldline establishment, see E. Digby Baltzell, *The Protestant Establishment: Aristocracy and Caste in America* (New York: Random House, 1964); William R. Hutchinson, ed., *Between the Times: The Travail of the Protestant Establishment in America, 1900–1960* (Cambridge, England: Cambridge University Press, 1989); and David Brooks, *Bobos in Paradise: The New Upper Class and How They Got There* (New York: Simon & Schuster, 2000).

3. Philip E. Hammond, *Religion and Personal Autonomy: The Third Disestablishment in America* (Columbia: University of South Carolina Press, 1992), 139. And to further complicate the matter, disestablishment has also occurred at varying rates in different regions of the United States and in different denominations. See Hammond, pp. 139–66.

4. Eldon G. Ernst, *Without Help or Hindrance: Religious Identity in American Culture*, 2nd ed. (Lanham, Md.: University Press of America, 1987), p. 151.

5. Hammond, *Religion and Personal Autonomy*, p. 10.

6. Will Herberg, *Protestant-Catholic-Jew: An Essay in American Religious Sociology*, rev. ed. (New York: Doubleday, 1960).

7. Wade Clark Roof and William McKinney, *American Mainline Religion: Its Changing Shape and Future* (New Brunswick, N.J.: Rutgers University Press, 1987); and Phillip E. Hammond, *Religion and Personal Autonomy: The Third Disestablishment in America* (Columbia: University of South Carolina Press, 1992).

8. According to a recent poll, 78% of Protestant clergy believe that the separation of church and state has "gone too far or in ways it was never intended to go." Only 13% agreed that the current practice of disestablishment "is right where it should be." Reported in *Religion Watch* 19, no. 9 (July 2004): p. 3.

9. Loren B. Mead, *The Once and Future Church: Reinventing the Congregation for a New Mission Frontier* (Bethesda, Md.: Alban Institute, 1991); and Stanley Hauerwas and William H. Willimon, *Resident Aliens: Life in the Christian Colony* (Nashville: Abingdon, 1989).

10. Paul Heelas, "Introduction: Detraditionalization and its Rivals," in *Detraditionalization: Critical Reflections on Authority and Identity*, ed. Paul Heelas, Scott Lash, and Paul Morris (Oxford, England and Cambridge, Mass.: Blackwell, 1996), p. 2.

11. Jackson W. Carroll and Wade Clark Roof, *Bridging Divided Worlds: Generational Cultures in Congregations* (San Francisco: Jossey-Bass, 2002), p. 52.

12. Heelas, "Introduction: Detraditionalization and Its Rivals," p. 2

13. Ibid., p. 4.

14. Ibid., p. 5.

15. Many intellectuals have written of this phenomenon as well. Books like Francis Fukuyama's *The End of History and the Last Man* (New York: Free Press, 1992); Christopher Lasch's *The Culture of Narcissism: American Life in an Age of Diminishing Expectations* (New York: Norton, 1978); Allen Bloom's *The Closing of the American Mind* (New York: Simon & Schuster, 1987); and Robert Bellah et al.'s *Habits of the Heart: Individualism and Commitment in American Life* (Berkeley: University of California Press, 1985) all document aspects of radical detraditionalization in American culture.

16. Heelas, p. 3.

17. Ibid., p. 10.

Chapter Three

1. The full story is told in Diana Butler Bass, *Strength for the Journey: A Pilgrimage of Faith in Community* (San Francisco: Jossey-Bass, 2002), pp. 223–60. I am quoting from David Fikes's sermon, found in *Strength*, p. 255.

2. Eric Hobsbawm, "Introduction: Inventing Traditions," in *The Invention of Tradition*, ed. Eric Hobsbawm and Terence Ranger (Cambridge, England: Cambridge University Press, 1983), pp. 1ff.

3. Danièle Hervieu-Léger, *Religion as a Chain of Memory*, trans. Simon Lee (New Brunswick, N.J.: Rutgers University Press, 2000), p. 87.

4. Alasdair MacIntyre, *After Virtue: A Study in Moral Theology*, 2nd ed. (Notre Dame, Ind.: University of Notre Dame Press, 1984), p. 222.

5. Kathryn Tanner, *Theories of Culture: A New Agenda for Theology,* Guides to Theological Inquiry (Minneapolis: Fortress Press, 1997), p. 163.

6. Hobsbawn, "Introduction: Inventing Traditions," p. 2.

7. John B. Thompson, "Tradition and Self in a Mediated World," in *Detraditionalization: Critical Reflections on Authority and Identity,* ed. Paul Heelas, Scott Lash, and Paul Morris (Oxford, England and Cambridge, Mass.: Blackwell, 1996), p. 93.

8. Hervieu-Léger, *Religion as a Chain,* p. 87.

9. Wade Clark Roof, *Spiritual Marketplace: Baby Boomers and the Remaking of American Religion* (Princeton, N.J.: Princeton University Press, 1999), p. 165.

10. Ibid., p. 165.

11. Hervieu-Léger, *Religion as a Chain,* p. 88.

12. Ibid.

13. From Georges Balandier, *LeDésordre. Éloge du mouvement* (Paris: Fayard, 1988); translated and summarized in Hervieu-Léger, *Religion as a Chain,* pp. 88–89.

14. These definitions are drawn from Hervieu-Léger, *Religion as a Chain of Memory.*

15. Ibid., p. 100.

16. Very little has been written about this switch. The most suggestive descriptions of the dynamic nature of tradition among American mainline Protestants are found in William Sachs and Thomas Holland, *Restoring the Ties That Bind: The Grassroots Transformation of the Episcopal Church* (New York: Church Publishing, 2003); Jackson W. Carroll, *Mainline to the Future: Congregations for the 21st Century* (Louisville: Westminster John Knox, 2000); and Marcus J. Borg, *The Heart of Christianity: Rediscovering a Life of Faith* (San Francisco: HarperSanFrancisco, 2003).

17. Roger Finke, "Innovative Returns to Traditions: Using Core Teachings as the Foundation for Innovative Accommodation," *Journal for the Scientific Study of Religion* 43, no. 1 (2004): p. 20.

18. Ibid., p. 29.

19. John Henry Newman, *Essay on the Development of Christian Doctrine* (Westminster, Md.: Christian Classics, 1968), p. 58.

20. Hobsbawn, "Introduction: Inventing Traditions," p. 1.

21. Ibid., pp. 4–5.

22. On tradition as a denominational strategy, see Adair T. Lummis, "Brand Name Identity in a Post-Denominational Age: Regional Leaders' Perspectives On Its Importance for Churches" (paper delivered at the

annual meetings of the Society for the Scientific Study of Religion, Columbus, Ohio, October 2001), available at http://hirr.hartsem.edu/bookshelf/lummis_article1.html. For retraditioning among younger adults, see Robert E. Webber, *The Younger Evangelicals: Facing the Challenges of the New World* (Grand Rapids, Mich.: Baker, 2002), esp. chap. 4, "History: From Ahistorical to Tradition," pp. 71–82; Colleen Carroll, *The New Faithful: Why Young Adults Are Embracing Christian Orthodoxy* (Chicago: Loyola Press, 2002); Diana Butler Bass, *Strength for the Journey*; and Lauren F. Winner, *Girl Meets God: On the Path to a Spiritual Life* (Chapel Hill, N.C.: Algonquin Books, 2002).

23. Zygmunt Bauman, "Morality in the Age of Contingency," in *Detraditionalization*, ed. Heelas et al., p. 51.

24. Hervieu-Léger, *Religion as a Chain*, p. 123.

25. Ibid., p. 125.

26. Paul Morris, "Community Beyond Tradition," in *Detraditionalization*, ed. Heelas et al., p. 224.

27. Dorothy C. Bass, "Congregations and the Bearing of Traditions," in James P. Wind and James W. Lewis, eds., *American Congregations, Volume 2: New Perspectives in the Study of Congregations* (Chicago: University of Chicago Press, 1994), p. 170.

28. Ibid., p. 188.

29. Jackson W. Carroll and Wade Clark Roof, eds., *Beyond Establishment: Protestant Identity in a Post-Protestant Age* (Louisville: Westminster John Knox, 1993), pp. 16–17.

30. Ibid., p. 18.

31. This idea of the congregation as a community of practice was informed by Etienne Wenger, *Communities of Practice: Learning, Meaning, and Identity* (Cambridge, England: Cambridge University Press, 1998).

32. Thompson, "Tradition and Self," in *Detraditionalization*, ed. Heelas et al., pp. 103–106.

33. Ibid., p. 106.

Chapter Four

1. Dietrich Bonhoffer, *The Cost of Discipleship*, rev. ed. (London: SCM Press, 1959), p. 36.

2. Ibid., p. 59.

3. Craig Dykstra, *Growing in the Life of Faith: Education and Christian Practices* (Louisville: Geneva Press, 1999), p. 3.

4. Jonathan R. Wilson, *Living Faithfully in a Fragmented World: Lessons for the Church from MacIntyre's* After Virtue; Christian Mission and Modern Culture (Harrisburg, Pa.: Trinity Press International, 1997).

5. Marcus J. Borg, *The Heart of Christianity: Rediscovering a Life of Faith* (San Francisco: HarperSanFrancisco, 2003), p. 188.

6. Zygmunt Bauman, "Morality in the Age of Contingency," in *Detraditionalization: Critical Reflections on Authority and Identity*, ed. Paul Heelas, Scott Lash, and Paul Morris (Oxford, England and Cambridge, Mass.: Blackwell, 1996), p. 51.

7. Nora Gallagher, *Things Seen and Unseen: A Year Lived in Faith* (New York: Knopf, 1998), p. 11.

8. Bauman, "Morality," p. 53.

9. As told in Gallagher, *Things Seen and Unseen* and Diana Butler Bass, *Strength for the Journey: A Pilgrimage of Faith in Community* (San Francisco: Jossey-Bass, 2002).

10. Dorothy C. Bass and Craig Dykstra, "Christian Practices and Congregational Education in Faith," in Michael Warren, ed., *Changing Churches: The Local Church and the Structures of Change* (Portland: Pastoral Press of Oregon Catholic Press, 2000); reprinted at http://www.resourcingchristianity.org.

11. Alasdair MacIntyre, *After Virtue: A Study in Moral Theology*, 2nd ed. (Notre Dame, Ind.: University of Notre Dame Press, 1984), p. 263.

12. Wilson, *Living Faithfully*, pp. 68–78. Luther E. Smith Jr. makes a similar argument in his *Intimacy and Mission: Intentional Community as Crucible for Radical Discipleship* (Scottdale, Pa.: Herald Press, 1994).

13. In some ways, the development of congregation-as-monastic-community echoes earlier styles of renewal in establishment Protestantism. For example, both the eighteenth-century Methodist movement and the nineteenth-century Oxford movement answered the challenges of denominational decline by reaching into the past and recovering historic Christian practices. In both cases, the entirety of the church (or the majority of the church) became a spiritually purposeful small group—or a monastic community. Now, of course, this "movement" impulse happens in a radically different context in a culturally fragmented world. However, seriousness around Christian practice may represent a contemporary expression of a vitality pattern native to this part of American

Protestantism. On the movement orientation and mainline vitality, see C. Kirk Hadaway and David A. Roozen, *Rerouting the Protestant Mainstream: Sources of Growth and Opportunities for Change* (Nashville: Abingdon, 1995), esp. chap. 6, "Mainstream Movements," pp. 109–123.

14. Dietrich Bonhoeffer, *Life Together* (New York: Harper & Row, 1954), p. 37.

15. L. Gregory Jones, *Embodying Forgiveness: A Theological Analysis* (Grand Rapids, Mich.: Wm. B. Eerdmans, 1995), p. 13.

16. Robert Wuthnow, *After Heaven: Spirituality in America Since the 1950s* (Berkeley: University of California Press, 1998), pp. 168–198. From my experience, most church-growth programs—from national movements like Willow Creek to local judicatory initiatives—are based on the assumption that Americans are religious seekers. While that assumption may have been the case twenty years ago, Wuthnow (and others) suggest that it is not the case today. Thus, despite the successes of some church-growth strategies, they are wedded to particular generational ideals that are increasingly less reflective of the experiences of younger Americans. For another example of this, see Robert E. Webber, *The Younger Evangelicals: Facing the Challenges of the New World* (Grand Rapids, Mich.: Baker, 2002).

17. Wuthnow, *After Heaven*, pp. 169, 170.

18. Dorothy C. Bass, ed., *Practicing Our Faith: A Way of Life for a Searching People* (San Francisco: Jossey-Bass, 1998), p. xi.

19. David D. Hall, ed., *Lived Religion in America* (Princeton, N.J.: Princeton University Press, 1997), p. xi.

20. Colleen McDannell, ed., *Religions of the United States in Practice*, Volume 1, Princeton Readings in Religions (Princeton, N.J.: Princeton University Press, 2001), pp. 2, 3. Emphasis hers.

21. Dykstra, *Growing in the Life of Faith*, p. 69.

22. Borg, *The Heart of Christianity*, p. 187.

23. Kathryn Tanner, "Theological Reflection and Christian Practices," in *Practicing Theology: Beliefs and Practices in Christian Life*, ed. Miroslav Volf and Dorothy C. Bass (Grand Rapids, Mich.: Wm. B. Eerdmans, 2001), pp. 228–230.

24. Dorothy C. Bass, "Introduction," in *Practicing Theology*, ed. Volf and Bass, p. 6.

25. Nora Gallagher, *Practicing Resurrection: A Memoir of Work, Doubt, Discernment, and Moments of Grace* (New York: Knopf, 1993), p. 148.

26. David A. Roozen, "Meeting Evangelicals Halfway," http://fact.hartsem.edu/topfindings/topicalfindings.htm.

27. Ibid.

28. Chart adapted from Bass, "Introduction" to *Practicing Theology;* Craig A. Dykstra and Dorothy C. Bass, "A Theological Understanding of Christian Practices," in *Practicing Theology;* Sarah Coakley, "Deepening Practices: Perspectives from Ascetical and Mystical Theology," in *Practicing Theology;* Kathryn Tanner, *Theories of Culture: A New Agenda for Theology.* Guides to Theological Inquiry (Minneapolis: Fortress Press, 1997).

Chapter Five

1. For the politicization of American religion, see Robert Wuthnow, *The Restructuring of American Religion* (Princeton, N.J.: Princeton University Press, 1985), and Patrick Allitt, *Religion in America Since 1945: A History* (New York: Columbia University Press, 2003).

2. See, for example, Ted Halsted and Michael Lind, *The Radical Center: The Future of American Politics* (New York: Doubleday, 2001); Mark Satin, *The Radical Middle: The Politics We Need Now* (New York: Westview, 2004); and John P. Avlon, *Independent Nation: How the Vital Center is Changing American Politics* (New York: Harmony, 2004).

3. William Sachs and Thomas Holland, *Restoring the Ties That Bind: The Grassroots Transformation of the Episcopal Church* (New York: Church Publishing, 2003), p. 87.

4. Ibid., p. 114.

5. Martin E. Marty, *Righteous Empire: The Protestant Experience in America* (New York: HarperCollins, 1977); a summary of the two-party idea can be found in Douglas Jacobsen and William Vance Trollinger Jr., eds., *Re-forming the Center: American Protestantism, 1900–Present* (Grand Rapids, Mich.: Wm. B. Eerdmans, 1998), pp. 1–14.

6. Robert Wuthnow, *The Restructuring of American Religion*, p. 215.

7. Ibid., pp. 239–240. One of the best examples of this analysis is James Davison Hunter, *Culture Wars: The Struggle to Define America* (New York: Basic Books, 1991).

8. Gary Dorrien, *The Making of American Liberal Theology: Idealism, Realism, and Modernity, 1900–1950* (Louisville: Westminster John Knox, 2003), p. 1.

9. Ibid.

10. Ibid., p. 3.

11. George M. Marsden, *Fundamentalism and American Culture: The Shaping of Twentieth-Century Evangelicalism, 1870–1920* (New York: Oxford University Press, 1980), p. 4.

12. See Diana Hochstedt Butler, *Standing Against the Whirlwind: Evangelical Episcopalians in Nineteenth-Century America* (New York: Oxford University Press, 1995).

13. William Sachs and Thomas Holland, "Conflict, Culture, and Institution: The Many Forms of Episcopal Conflict," chap. 3 in *Restoring the Ties That Bind*, pp. 79–115.

14. Bradley J. Longfield, *The Presbyterian Controversy: Fundamentalists, Modernists, and Moderates* (New York: Oxford University Press, 1993).

15. Some of the most engaging of these stories include: Randall Balmer, *Growing Pains: Learning to Love My Father's Faith* (Grand Rapids, Mich.: Brazos Press, 2001); Diana Butler Bass, *Strength for the Journey: A Pilgrimage of Faith in Community* (San Francisco: Jossey-Bass, 2002); Betty Smartt Carter, *Home is Always the Place You Just Left* (Brewster, Mass.: Paraclete, 2003); Mary Cartledgehayes, *Grace: A Memoir* (New York: Crown, 2003); Patrick Henry, *The Ironic Christian's Companion: Finding the Marks of God's Grace in the World* (New York: Riverhead, 1999); Anne Lamott, *Traveling Mercies: Some Thoughts on Faith* (New York: Random House, 1999); and Phyllis Tickle, *The Shaping of A Life: A Spiritual Landscape* (New York: Doubleday, 2001).

16. Jacobsen and Trollinger, *Re-forming the Center;* see esp. Mark Ellingsen's essay, "Narrative Theology and the Pre-Enlightenment Ethos of the American Protestant Center," pp. 421–444.

17. Jacobsen and Trollinger, "Conclusion," in *Re-forming the Center,* p. 470.

18. Butler Bass, *Strength for the Journey,* p. 149.

19. See chart in chapter 1.

20. Larry McMurtry, "Life Is a Foreign Country," *New York Times Book Review* (September 8, 1985), http://www.nytimes.com/books/98/04/19/specials/tyler-tourist.html; reviewing Anne Tyler, *The Accidental Tourist* (New York: Knopf, 1985).

21. McMurtry, "Life Is a Foreign Country."

22. Robert Wuthnow, *After Heaven: Spirituality in America Since the 1950s* (Berkeley: University of California Press, 1998), p. 40.

23. Lamott, *Traveling Mercies,* p. 3.

24. T. S. Eliot, *Little Gidding*, in *Collected Poems, 1909–1962* (London: Faber & Faber, 1963), p. 222.

25. Nathan O. Hatch, *The Democratization of American Religion* (New Haven, Conn.: Yale University Press, 1991); Robert N. Bellah et al, *Habits of the Heart: Individualism and Commitment in American Life* (Berkeley: University of California Press, 1985).

26. Marcus Borg's book *The Heart of Christianity: Rediscovering a Life of Faith* (San Francisco: HarperSanFrancisco, 2003) describes this way of understanding faith as a "new paradigm" of Christianity, but he continues to emphasize this cluster of characteristics as primary acts and beliefs of individuals and only hints at the idea of congregations being practicing communities.

27. Wade Clark Roof, *Spiritual Marketplace: Baby Boomers and the Remaking of American Religion* (Princeton, N.J.: Princeton University Press, 1999), p. 75.

28. Ibid.

29. Nancey Murphy convincing argues this in *Beyond Liberalism and Fundamentalism: How Modern and Postmodern Philosophy Set the Theological Agenda*, Rockwell Lecture Series (Harrisburg, Pa.: Trinity Press International, 1996).

30. John B. Webster, "Theology After Liberalism?" in *Theology After Liberalism: A Reader*, ed. John Webster and George P. Schner, Blackwell Readings in Modern Theology (Oxford, England: Blackwell, 2000), pp. 54–55. The early "manifesto" of postliberalism is George A. Lindbeck, *The Nature of Doctrine: Religion and Theology in a Postliberal Age* (Philadelphia: Westminster, 1984).

31. Webster, "Theology After Liberalism?" p. 55.

32. Dave Tomlinson, *The Post-Evangelical* (El Cajon, Calif.: emergentYS, 2003), pp. 17, 11. Tomlinson's original work was published in England in 1995 and has since had a huge impact on American evangelicals. For the best American expression of post-evangelicalism, see Brian D. McLaren, *A New Kind of Christian: A Tale of Two Friends on a Spiritual Journey* (San Francisco: Jossey-Bass, 2001).

33. It may not disappear completely because it is now a three-generation inheritance from the fundamentalist-modernist controversy. Several generations of American Protestants have been schooled to think in these categories.

34. Jacobsen and Trollinger, "Conclusion," in *Re-forming the Center*, p. 471.

Chapter Six

1. Urban T. Holmes III, *Ministry and Imagination* (New York: Seabury Press, 1976), p. 109.

2. Ibid., p. 117.

3. Ibid., p. 118.

4. Ibid.

5. The story of Trinity Episcopal Church is told in Diana Butler Bass, *Strength for the Journey: A Pilgrimage of Faith in Community* (San Francisco: Jossey-Bass, 2002), pp. 189–222. The quotes are found on pp. 192, 202, and 219.

6. David A. Hogue, Remembering the Future/Imaging the Past: Story, Ritual, and the Human Brain (Cleveland: Pilgrim Press, 2003), pp. 42, 44.

7. Ibid., p. 45.

8. Ibid., pp. 181–96.

9. Holmes, *Ministry and Imagination*, pp. 123–28.

10. Ibid., p. 102.

11. The story of the failure to rework tradition in light of new circumstances is ably developed by Roger Finke and Rodney Stark in *The Churching of America, 1776–1990: Winners and Losers in Our Religious Economy* (New Brunswick, N.J.: 1992).

12. Holmes, *Ministry and Imagination*, p. 103.

13. These developments are surveyed in John Navone, S.J., *Seeking God in Story* (Collegeville, Minn.: Liturgical Press, 1990).

14. See Brad J. Kallenberg, "The Master Argument of MacIntyre's *After Virtue*" in Nancey Murphy et al, eds., *Virtues and Practices in the Christian Tradition: Christian Ethics after MacIntrye* (Harrisburg, Pa.: Trinity Press International, 1997), p. 28.

15. Navone, *Seeking God in Story,* p. xvi.

16. Barbara Wheeler, "Editor's Foreword," in James F. Hopewell, *Congregation: Stories and Structures* (Philadelphia: Fortress Press, 1987), p. xii.

17. Dorothy Bass, "Practicing Theology in the Congregation," *Congregations* (Winter 2004), p. 24. Found also at http://www.alban.org/ShowArticle.asp?ID=209.

18. Ernest Kurtz and Katherine Ketcham, *The Spirituality of Imperfection: Storytelling and the Search for Meaning* (New York: Bantam, reissue, 2002), p. 8.

19. Personal conversation, March 2004.

20. Holmes, *Ministry and Imagination*, p. 135.

21. T. S. Eliot, *Little Gidding* in *Collected Poems, 1909–1962* (London: Faber & Faber, 1963), p. 222; G. K. Chesterton, *Orthodoxy* (New York: Doubleday, 1990; reprint of 1908 edition [New York: Dodd & Mead]), p. 15.

22. Howard Gardner, *Leading Minds: An Anatomy of Leadership* (New York: Basic Books, 1996), pp. 9, ix.

23. David Fleming, "Narrative Leadership: Using the Power of Stories," from *Strategy and Leadership* 29, no. 4 (2001): pp. 34–36, viewed at http://emergingleadersinstitute.org.

24. On the power of testimony, see Thomas Hoyt, Jr., "Testimony," in *Practicing Our Faith: A Way of Life for a Searching People*, ed. Dorothy C. Bass (San Francisco: Jossey-Bass, 1997), pp. 91–103. On the experience of Church of the Redeemer, see Lillian F. Daniel, "The Practice of Testimony at the Church of the Redeemer, United Church of Christ, New Haven, Connecticut," unpublished Doctor of Ministry thesis, Hartford Theological Seminary, March 2004.

25. Gardner, *Leading Minds*, p. xi.

26. From *The Way to Love: The Last Meditations of Anthony de Mello* (New York: Image Books, 1991), p. 4.

Questions for Reflection and Study

Prepared by Joseph Stewart-Sicking

Chapter 1: A New Old Church

1. Chapter 1 suggested that American Protestantism is entering a new historical period, characterized by the emergence of the *intentional congregation*. What signs have you seen of this change in the wider Church? In your own church? What excites you about this emerging pattern?

2. Chapter 1 also discussed different periods in the history of American congregations (see chart, p. 17). In which period was your church founded? What remains from this and the intervening periods (architecture, groups, parishioners, organization)? What are the resources these bring to the continuing history of your congregation?

Chapter 2: Just the Way It Is

1. How have you encountered disestablishment and detraditioning in your own congregation?

2. Think back to the challenges your church has faced in the past decade. How might it be different to see these challenges in light of these cultural changes rather than as the fault of troublesome staff, leaders, parishioners, or denominations?

Chapter 3: Tradition, Tradition!

1. Chapter 3 made a distinction between customs ("actions in accordance with precedent") and tradition ("an historically extended, socially embodied argument" about true discipleship). Think of the many areas of your church's communal life: worship, gatherings, ministries, events. What are examples of customs that are important to your church? What longer Christian traditions do these customs reflect? Do the customs reflect your current understanding of these traditions? If not, what new customs might your church be called to?

2. How do most people in your church talk about tradition (a deposit, a continuity of appearance, an irrelevant vestige, a living argument with the past)? How might your approach to your communal life be different if you adopted the stance of fluid retraditioning? What might you be able to accomplish with this idea that other ideas of tradition could not?

3. Chapter 3 suggests that retraditioning is a congregational journey made from the grass-roots up. Bearing in mind that this can take some unexpected forms—including arguments—what are some signs you have seen in your church of retraditioning?

4. Tradition implies conversation with the past leaders of the Church. Who is a figure in the Church's history who has been a good conversation partner for you? How could you share this spiritual friend with others?

Chapter 4: Practice Makes Pilgrims

1. Chapter 4 examines Christian practices: activities pursued over time that develop character and which constitute a way of life. While many practices may happen "accidentally," they require intentionality to provide growth. What practices are central to your church's vision of Christian discipleship? How have you become more intentional about these practices? How might you be more intentional in cultivating them? What are some concrete examples of how you have grown through pursuing these practices?

2. Not every practice is Christian (e.g., Paul says that several Jewish practices are no longer binding on Christians in the same way.) How do you discern whether a practice is Christian? How are your practices linked to Scripture and the traditions of the Church?

3. Not every practice is meant for every Christian. How do you discern which practices are part of your church's vocation? How does your congregation help its members discern which practices match their gifts?

4. Since practices constitute a way of life, they are "thick"— they lead back and forth into one another and involve the entirety of one's life. How does your congregation foster seeing practice as a way of life? What pathways are there for participation in one practice to lead to participation in another (especially in light of how your ministries are structured)?

Chapter 5: Seeing the Mainline Again

1. Chapter 5 identifies how stories about the Church are often framed according to a dominant story of conservative-liberal conflict. To examine the effect of this discourse on your view of the Church, consider the following exercise, suitable for use in a church board or staff meeting:

- Gather news coverage about mainline churches, especially your own denomination from periodicals and the internet (Google News is a helpful tool for this)—and don't forget to include denominational periodicals. Cut out the headlines and any images and attach them to newsprint. Hang the newsprint around the room and allow participants to tour the display with pen and paper, noting the actors and common themes.

- In a small group, discuss the actors and themes people saw. Who do these stories say that Christians are? Do these stories affect how you approach living as a church? Do they represent the actors and stories that are important in the life of your congregation? How might you work at spreading different stories?

An interesting variant on this exercise is to use only those materials which people encounter in your church and office.

2. Chapter 5 also suggested that greater intentionality tends to blur the liberal-conservative distinction. How have you seen this phenomenon? Why do you think this happens?

Chapter 6: I Love to Tell the Story

1. Chapter 6 suggested that the stories we tell about ourselves dictate our actions and perceptions. The following group exercise helps uncover the stories that shape your church's perception of itself:

- Gather church bulletins and newsletters from the past six months and cut out the headlines and pictures. Attach these to newsprint and post the newsprint around the walls of the room in which the group is meeting. Have participants go around the room and take notes for discussion.
- Returning to the center of the room for discussion, address the following questions: Who do they say that you are? Who do they say God is? What do they say ministry is? What do they say is happening in the Church? Where do they say that God is present?

Consider doing this exercise in conjunction with the news exercise for Chapter 5. What discrepancies do you see between the stories you want to tell about yourself as a church and those that you encounter in the news? What are the effects of looking at your church as part of the news stories versus your own stories?

2. Often the dominant stories of decline and conflict can mask what is happening in a church. Look back at the past year in your church's life. What are some examples of exceptions to these dominant narratives? How did they happen? How might you nurture these stories?

About the Cover Art

"Lord Build This House" by Leonard Freeman

I painted "Lord Build This House" after hearing a sermon based on Psalm 127:1 which says, "Except the Lord build the house they that build it labor in vain." The painting is filled with symbolic imagery that is based on scriptural excerpts from the Bible. These symbolisms are:

The foundation upon which the worshippers are standing represent the LORD Jesus Christ, our rock of salvation. (Isaiah 28:16, 1 Corinthians 3:11)

The fields of wheat stretching beyond the horizon represent the ripe harvest Jesus spoke of concerning people in need of salvation. (Luke 10:2)

The predominant colors of *blue* (sky), *white* (clouds), *purple* (horizon), and *gold* (wheat), represent the majestic colors of royalty worn by Mordecai (Esther's cousin) after the king honored him. (Esther 8:15)

The moving clouds rising up from the distance represent *God's* command to his people to follow the cloud that He provided to lead them to the Promised Land. (Exodus 13:21)

The building, whose many parts are being fitly joined together, represent the different denominations of Christians who are being brought together through their common love of Jesus Christ. (Ephesians 2:21)

The stars in the sky from which the building is descending represent heaven, *God's* domain, the place of origin for all blessings. (Deuteronomy 10:14)

The shadows cast on the front of the building represent the light of the *Bright and Morning Star* as it shines *God's* approval upon the worshipping saints. (Revelation 22:16)

The five columns represent the five-fold ministry: *Apostles, Prophets, Evangelists, Pastors and Teachers.* (Ephesians 4:11)

The twelve windows (six on each side of building), represent each of the twelve apostles who followed Jesus during his ministry. (Matthew 10:2-4)

The four doors in the front of the church represent the four books of the Gospel *(Matthew, Mark, Luke, and John)* We enter into the New Testament era through these four books.

The three parts of the steeple represent the Trinity: Father, Son, and Holy Spirit. (Matthew 28:19)

The cross, the last piece to descend from heaven, represent our risen Savior as he honors his promise to return, receiving the believers unto himself. (Acts 1:11)

For information on Leonard Freeman, Artist, visit www.leonardfreemanart.com.

About the Author

Diana Butler Bass is senior research fellow and director of the Project on Congregations of Intentional Practice, a Lilly Endowment–funded research study of vital mainline Protestant churches, at Virginia Theological Seminary in Alexandria, Virginia. From 1994–2000, she wrote a weekly column on American religion for the New York Times Syndicate. She is the author of *Broken We Kneel: Reflections on Faith and Citizenship* (Jossey-Bass, 2004); *Strength for the Journey: A Pilgrimage of Faith in Community* (Jossey-Bass, 2002), a *Publishers Weekly* Notable Book of 2002; and *Standing against the Whirlwind: Evangelical Episcopalians in the Nineteenth Century* (Oxford University Press, 1995).

She holds a Ph.D. in American religious history from Duke University, a master's of theology from Gordon-Conwell Theological Seminary, and a bachelor's degree from Westmont College. She has taught at Duke University, Westmont College, the University of California at Santa Barbara, Macalester College, and Rhodes College. In 1998–1999, she spent a sabbatical as a research associate for the Zacchaeus Project, an ethnographic survey of more than 300 Episcopal congregations.

She is a member of Church of the Epiphany, an Episcopal parish in downtown Washington, D.C., and lives in Alexandria, Virginia, with her husband and children.